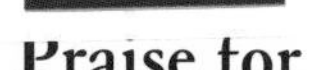

Praise for
Conversation—The Sacred Art: Practicing Presence in an Age of Distraction

"This is a book you will linger with—as you do, after a meal, over a cup of coffee, when the conversation is as nourishing as the food."

—**Sharon Daloz Parks**, co-author, *Common Fire: Leading Lives of Commitment in a Complex World*; former associate professor, Harvard Divinity School and Weston Jesuit School of Theology

"Exquisite.... Diane Millis writes with the grace, wisdom and caring of a wise and skillful spiritual director, leading us all to touch the sacred within ourselves, within others and in the midst of all of our conversations."

—**Rabbi Amy Eilberg**, Jay Phillips Center for Interfaith Learning, St. Paul, Minnesota

"A beautiful book filled with exquisite insights, practices and stories. They illuminate our heart and mind and awaken us to Presence."

—**Imam Jamal Rahman**, author, *Spiritual Gems of Islam: Insights & Practices from the Qur'an, Hadith, Rumi & Muslim Teaching Stories to Enlighten the Heart & Mind*

"Integrates the author's intensive study of spiritual guidance with her personal and professional experiences [and] offers both inspiration and practical guidance to restore the art of conversation as a sacred activity."

—**Dr. Aostre N. Johnson**, professor of education, Saint Michael's College

"Plunges us into that holy space from which we can connect with God, with ourselves and especially with others at a depth we would have thought impossible. Our conversations will never be the same after reading this book—they will be infinitely richer."

—**John Backman**, author, *Why Can't We Talk?: Christian Wisdom on Dialogue as a Habit of the Heart*

"Diane Millis knows that our conversation reveals us to others, and, done right—caring more important than understanding, talking balanced with restraint and periodic silence—reveals to us depths we didn't know we have. She has learned much from others, and shares her own practical wisdom, most forcefully and poignantly demonstrated in the transition from 'broken apart' to 'breaking open.'"

—**Patrick Henry**, retired executive director, Collegeville Institute for Ecumenical and Cultural Research; author, *The Ironic Christian's Companion: Finding the Marks of God's Grace in the World*

"Profound ... teaches us how conversation—listening, speaking, and even silence—can help us genuinely connect to others and even ourselves through our hearts, deepening our relationships, recognizing God within us and God between us."

—**Sara Hacala**, author, *Saving Civility: 52 Ways to Tame Rude, Crude, and Attitude for a Polite Planet*

Conversation —the sacred art

Practicing Presence in an Age of Distraction

Diane M. Millis, PhD

Foreword by Rev. Tilden Edwards, PhD

Walking Together, Finding the Way®

SKYLIGHT PATHS®
PUBLISHING
Woodstock, Vermont

Conversation—The Sacred Art
Practicing Presence in an Age of Distraction

2013 Quality Paperback Edition, First Printing

Page 154 constitutes a continuation of this copyright page.

Library of Congress Cataloging-in-Publication Data

Millis, Diane M., 1962-
Conversation, the sacred art : practicing presence in an age of distraction / by Diane M. Millis, PhD ; foreword by the Rev. Tilden Edwards.
pages cm
Includes bibliographical references.
ISBN 978-1-59473-474-8
1. Conversation—Religious aspects. 2. Communication—Religious aspects. 3. Awareness—Religious aspects. 4. Attention—Religious aspects. 5. Distraction (Psychology)—Religious aspects. 6. Listening—Religious aspects. I. Title.
BL629.5.C67M55 2013
205'.672--dc23

2012050553

10 9 8 7 6 5 4 3 2 1

Manufactured in the United States of America
Cover and Interior Design: Heather Pelham
Cover Art: © SchneiderStockImages, modified by Heather Pelham

SkyLight Paths Publishing is creating a place where people of different spiritual traditions come together for challenge and inspiration, a place where we can help each other understand the mystery that lies at the heart of our existence.

SkyLight Paths sees both believers and seekers as a community that increasingly transcends traditional boundaries of religion and denomination—people wanting to learn from each other, *walking together, finding the way*.

Walking Together, Finding the Way®
Published by SkyLight Paths Publishing
A Division of LongHill Partners, Inc.
Sunset Farm Offices, Route 4, P.O. Box 237
Woodstock, VT 05091
Tel: (802) 457-4000 Fax: (802) 457-4004
www.skylightpaths.com

For Mark and Ryan

We mark with light in the memory
the few interviews we have had
with souls that made our souls wiser,
that spoke what we thought,
that told us what we knew,
that gave us leave to be
what we truly are.

—*Ralph Waldo Emerson*

CONTENTS

FOREWORD

Listen well
Speak truth
Be peace

These simple words, written to me on a bookmark from the author, say so much about this invaluable book. They advocate the kind of intention that we and the whole world need to bring to conversations at every level if we are to fulfill the promise of human community and minimize soul-killing and conflict-inducing conversations.

The great practical value of this book is that it not only gives us an overarching sacred intention for our conversations, but it also provides concrete and tested ways to *carry out* that intention. Diane M. Millis's goal is to help us find a way to approach conversation as a spiritual practice and subsequently approach each other's lives as works of art. Yet this approach is challenged by so much in our culture, keeping us on the unsatisfying, fearful, and role playing surface with one another.

Dr. Millis has a wonderful practice of placing a glass bowl of water in the middle of a group, symbolizing a still, contemplative container that invites us to see the reflection of our own and other's deepest truths together. To reach such depth we need to listen and speak from our spiritual heart rather than from our ego self-centeredness and stereotyping thoughts. We need to be open to our own personal depths as well as those of others in the conversation, and we need to hear what is presented to us in the sacred space between us. Time for a listening silence is needed as well as space for speaking, since the fullness of awareness is found beyond words.

From my many years of structuring small groups in the ecumenical Shalem Institute's contemplative leadership programs, I can attest to the priceless value of this basic way of being with others. We give a great deal of weight to dropping behind the self-centered and stereotyping ego level so that we can listen from the deepest place in us—our spiritual heart.

In this sense, our spiritual heart is more than the place of our feelings and will; it is also the place of a different faculty of *knowing* in us, the place of a more direct, intuitive awareness. In contemplative terms, we could speak of the heart as the place of deepest intimacy with the divine Presence. It is the place where our receptive spirit blends with the Holy Spirit's movements and we find ourselves hearing and responding from the fruit of that blending.

In order for our heart to be ascendant, we need to approach it with great openness, clinging to nothing but our desire for loving truth. We must be willing to live in the fresh, immediate, living moment, released from our securing, controlling views, and give our trust to the larger sacred Presence. We need to bring to the moment only our desire for whatever wisdom and compassion is meant for us to receive or offer.

In my experience, such a shared intention in a group, lived out in a carefully structured process that gives that intention maximum opportunity to be fulfilled, bears enormous fruit for group members—sometimes life-transforming fruit.

Diane Millis provides such a crucial structure, with many witnesses to its incredible value for people's awareness of their deeper selves, one another, and the sacred reality alive between them. Because she has formed interfaith groups whose members don't share the same religious vocabulary, she has used helpful language for the sacred that can cross many boundaries. That, in itself, is a great contribution of this book, since interfaith, as well as "questioner" faith, relationships are so important for our shared well-being today. The process she provides brings people together across boundaries at the heart level, allowing so much fuller sharing together. She treats such collective deep listening as an act of love, listening for sacred currents beneath the surface stream of life.

Listening from the heart assumes the dignity of each person as a unique image of God. It assumes that within us we can access particular loving wisdom meant for us and others, wisdom that is compatible with the depth wisdom of our religious traditions. As Dr. Millis says, "Each of our lives is a source of sacred truth." The price of such access is letting go of our self-centeredness and vulnerably opening the door to our larger, truer self in the sacred, loving Light. When we're empowered to do that, we find the inner authority of our own deep awareness and its creative and compassionate callings.

Such a way of being together also connects with the wide-scale rise of one-on-one spiritual companioning in many churches and spiritual centers in recent decades, as well as with the rise of small group spiritual direction. Millis shows us the value of a wider range of possible heart-centered conversation groups today.

Think what a difference it could make both inside and outside the religious world if such listening and responding from the heart were more widespread. So many human conflicts and misunderstandings flow from fearful, over-securing, stereotyping ego centeredness. When we can let our egos become functional vessels of our deeper heart-centered awareness, rather than the ultimate definers of who we and others are, there is so much more revelation and compassion available to us in our relationships.

Diane Millis's passion for helping us relate to ourselves, one another, and the divine Presence on a deeper level has led to her valuable research, teaching, and culminating articulation in this book of how we can be together in a crucial way for our own and for others' sake, and ultimately for the peace of the world. What she offers us is both a mature understanding of who we most deeply are and how we can bring that refreshing and liberating depth into our relationships. I expect that everyone who reads this book will be left with a larger sense of how conversation can become a soul-inspiring sacred art.

Rev. Tilden Edwards, PhD
Founder and Senior Fellow
Shalem Institute for Spiritual Formation

INTRODUCTION

When is the last time that you had a great conversation, a conversation which wasn't just two intersecting monologues, which is what passes for conversation a lot in this culture? But when had you last a great conversation, in which you overheard yourself saying things that you never knew you knew? That you heard yourself receiving from somebody words that absolutely found places within you that you thought you had lost and a sense of an event of a conversation that brought the two of you on to a different plane? And then fourthly, a conversation that continued to sing in your mind for weeks afterwards, you know? I've had some of them recently, and it's just absolutely amazing, like, as we would say at home, they are food and drink for the soul.

—*John O'Donohue,* On Being

I accompanied my husband, Mark, to dinner that evening with mixed feelings. I anticipated yet another night filled with conversations focused on health care, interspersed with snippets of talk about children or upcoming vacations. Since I didn't work in health care and I didn't have children at the time, I hoped I might find myself seated next to someone who would ask me a question other than the conventional, "What do you do for a living?" Perhaps this would be the night that conversational fairy dust would fall on my dinner companions, and they would inquire, "So what's giving you joy in your life these days?" As it turned out, no one asked me anything out of the ordinary. Instead, the fairy dust landed on me. Rather than waiting to be engaged in a conversation I found meaningful, I sought to engage others in one. Rather than limit ourselves to a superficial exchange, I tried a different tactic.

I felt emboldened and inspired by some reading I'd been doing in the *Rule of Benedict* on the practice of hospitality: "All guests who present themselves are to be welcomed as Christ" (53:1). I liked the sensibility of that. I felt challenged to consider how I might welcome each and every person I met as if he or she were Jesus. How would my conversations with others change if I truly believed that each person I encountered, from the cashier at the grocery store to my husband's colleagues at a dinner party, was a divine being? The answer was clear.

I would let go of my agenda and my expectations for conversations—the hope that others would notice me and delight in what I brought to the interaction. I would turn my intention from my ego's need to try to impress others and focus my attention on noticing the spark of divinity within each person at the table, including myself. I would set aside judgments and assumptions such as "all that people in health care want to do is talk about their work." I would try to learn and discover more about those seated at my table by asking questions about where they were finding currents of deeper meaning in their lives.

Looking back on that particular evening more than twenty years later, I recognize that I was just beginning to discover that conversation can be a sacred art. Although the words we exchange in a conversation are important and should be chosen with great care, conversation is about far more than words. Conversation is a way of being.

THE GIFTS OF CONVERSATION

Our conversations have the potential to nourish our souls. As a child, I witnessed the careful preparations my mother would make for our evening meals and holiday gatherings. For her, these occasions were about far more than preparing food. In fact, she devoted as much time to setting the table and creating a beautiful centerpiece as she did to cooking. My fondest memories were those occasions when people lingered at the table immersed in conversation long after the meal was finished.

A good conversation, like a good meal, is something we continue to savor over time. For those of us who live in the twenty-first century's digitalized world, we feel as if we have far less time to savor much, whether food, relationships, or conversations. Many of us find that in our effort to maintain a breadth of connection, we compromise the depth of our connections. We often feel distracted, as we struggle to keep up with all the messages that fill our screens, unable to bring our full attention to any single encounter, let alone have ample time to reflect on them. Jon Kabat-Zinn, a teacher of mindfulness practice, believes that time to reflect and cultivate attention is "no longer a luxury, but a lifeline back to what is most meaningful in our lives." In his book, *Coming to Our Senses*, he reports the consequences of not devoting ample time to reflection: "These assaults on our nervous system continually stimulate and foster desire and agitation rather than contentedness and calmness. They foster reaction rather than communion, discord rather than accord or concord, acquisitiveness rather than feeling whole and complete as we are."[1] More and more of us are feeling a need to disconnect selectively from our phones, pads, and computers in order to reconnect with our experiences, inner lives, and relationships.

Many of us want to retrieve what we feel we have lost since constant connectivity became a reality in our lives, for example, time for reflection and quiet without an expectation of continual availability. We would like to cultivate habits that help us be more fully present to one another. In a recent article, MIT professor Sherry Turkle observes, "When we communicate on our digital devices, we learn different habits. As we ramp up the volume and velocity of online connections, we start to expect faster answers. To get these, we ask one another simpler questions; we dumb down our communications, even on the most important matters."[2] We want to reclaim the foundational importance of conversation in our lives.

Conversation is the most delightful activity in our lives.
—Michel Montaigne

Great conversations are enlivening. We feel fully alive as we engage in a really good conversation. We are riveted to what is being revealed in this moment—losing track of concerns about what happened before or may happen afterward. In her book, *Turning to One Another: Simple Conversations to Restore Hope to the Future*, Margaret Wheatley reminds us that "human conversation is the most ancient and easiest way to cultivate the conditions for change—personal change, community and organizational change, planetary change. If we can sit together and talk about what's important to us, we begin to come alive. We share what we see, what we feel, and we listen to what others see and feel."[3]

Great conversations are enlightening. "Conversation is the natural way that we think together."[4] As we converse with one another, we have the opportunity to learn about a reality far bigger than our own and to learn more about ourselves. When another person deeply listens to us, rather than advising or analyzing us, it increases the likelihood that we will speak the truth of our heart. We hear ourselves saying things that we didn't know we knew or thought we had forgotten.

Great conversations are encouraging. Wheatley reminds us that "courage" comes from the Old French word for heart (*cuer*): "We develop courage for those things that speak to our heart. Our courage grows for things that affect us deeply, things that open our hearts."[5] When another person speaks from the core of his or her being to the core of our being, we are encouraged. When another invites us to speak the truth of our hearts, we have the opportunity to hear ourselves speak our truth, and our courage grows.

Great conversations are enjoyable. Regardless of the topic, one of the primary fruits of a great conversation is joy. Some of the most difficult periods in our lives can be punctuated with joy by the caring conversation partners who share their attention, receptivity, and compassion with us. Through our conversations, we can give and receive joy as well as learn more about the source of joy within one another.

I've devoted the majority of my adult life to learning and teaching about conversation. My undergraduate and graduate studies focused on communication theory and research—in interpersonal relationships, small groups, organizations, and especially in families. My fascination with conversation emerged from the indelible impact that my parent's divorce had on my life. As a result, I felt called to teach about the knowledge, communication skills, and attitudes that had the potential to strengthen and enrich all relationships, particularly marriages. I dedicated many years to teaching courses such as family communication or family spirituality in college and university classrooms. I delighted as more and more students sought me out after class or during office hours to explore their big questions. In order to become better equipped for these ad hoc conversations, I experienced another calling to train in the ministry of spiritual direction.

Learning the art of spiritual direction introduced me to a way of listening and being present in conversation that I hadn't encountered through my academic studies. Contemplative listening, or what's often referred to as listening in stereo, challenged me to listen deeply *within* as I listened to others. I began to grow in my awareness of the sacred Presence between me and others in a conversation as I attended to the deep stirrings within my own heart while paying attention to the deep stirrings in another's heart. I began to see that the skills and attitudes I had learned in my training as a spiritual director were never intended to be limited to a one-hour session with a directee. I felt challenged to practice spiritual companioning as *a way of being in conversation* with all whom I encountered. As I strived to listen from the depth of my heart in my everyday conversations and invite others to speak from the depth of theirs, I found that I was engaging in a spiritual practice: the sacred art of conversation.

Spiritual living evolves out of response to a sacred invitation. I believe that God is continually revealing God's self to us. This gift of God's communication occurs in and through every dimension of our lives. Therefore, it is possible for human communication with God to occur in and through the whole array of words, actions, objects, events, and relationships in our daily life. Each and every moment of our lives invites us to appreciate and pay attention to this gift of revelation. This sacred Presence infuses all aspects of our lives and all of our conversations. To think of conversation as a sacred art challenges us to imagine all the conversations in which we participate, from the acquaintance we run into at Target to the dialogue for which we've spent weeks in preparation, as a potentially sacred conversation.

The original meaning of the word "conversation" is the action of living or having one's being among persons. Practicing the sacred art of conversation is not just a matter of developing more skills. Conversation, like any sacred art, cannot be reduced to a checklist of do's and don'ts: "listen deeply," "respect silence," "ask good questions." Checklists tempt us to criticize ourselves and others in order to assess how we measure up to the prescribed criteria. Rather than being overly concerned with how we're doing, we want to try to appreciate and consider: how is mystery being revealed in this activity? As we engage in conversations with one another, we ask: how is mystery being revealed in what is transpiring between us?

Structure of This Book

In the following pages, I offer inspiration, guidance, and wisdom from an array of faith traditions for increasing our capacity to be present attentively to the sacred within us as we encounter the sacred between us. In Part One, "What Is the Sacred Art of Conversation?" we'll look at three dimensions of a conversation: encountering the sacred within ourselves, within others, and between us. In Part Two, "Gateways for Conversation," we'll consider topics and approaches for enriching our everyday conversations with others: reflecting upon and sharing the stories of our journeys, noticing and naming in our daily lives what stirs and moves us deeply, and discerning what gives our life purpose and meaning. In Part Three, "Practicing the Sacred Art of Conversation," we'll explore how to balance our inner and outer awareness as we engage in conversation, how to increase our receptivity to all that we encounter in a conversation, and how to cultivate our capacity to both listen and respond compassionately to others. In the closing section of the book, "The Sacred Art of Conversation in Community," we'll consider processes for facilitating the sacred art of conversation in small groups and communities. In the first appendix, you'll be introduced to a set of contemplative practices for conversations: stillness and centering, sacred reading, storytelling, compassionate listening and responding. In the second, you'll learn about some guiding principles and questions for appreciatively focused conversations, and in the third, you'll find conversation catalysts for sustaining conversations over time.

AN INVITATION

Each of us is on a journey. A journey does not presume a particular path, give preference to a particular faith tradition, or prescribe a particular theology. Each of us is trying to make meaning of who God is or is not for us, and how our understanding of what we hold sacred affects our relationship with ourselves, others, and the world in which we live. The perspective I bring to my writing is that of a committed Christian in the Roman Catholic tradition. My Christian faith has been deeply enriched by my encounter with other traditions. John Dunne, in his book, *The Way of All the Earth*, describes the adventure of *passing over* to other religious traditions and then *passing back* to one's own. Walking in someone else's "religious moccasins" potentially increases our understanding of other traditions and deepens our appreciation for our own. In writing this book, my intention has been to use language and concepts from my own tradition as well as understandings of the Divine that I have learned from other traditions.

Throughout the book, my aim is to broaden and deepen the way we think about conversation. Rather than hold up some conversations as sacred and others as not, I'd like us to imagine together how we might bring a greater intentionality and willingness to practice this sacred art in more of our conversations. What you will find in the following chapters is not a systematic account of the world's faith traditions and what they have to say about enriching conversation, deepening relationships, and cultivating community. Instead, I'm eager to introduce you to some of my favorite conversation partners: contemporary and historic wisdom figures from an array of traditions and contexts who have shaped my understanding of conversation as a sacred art. You will also read about my own journey, not because it's particularly interesting, but because I want to underscore the principle that each of our lives is a source of sacred truth. By sharing and showing you the ways that I am learning to pay attention to the truth being revealed in my own life, I hope that you will find yourself paying greater attention to the truth being revealed in yours and invite others to do the same.

As I wrote this book, my dear friend Tawanna e-mailed me the following: "As I read your chapters, I feel as if I'm in a conversation on all levels—I'm learning more about conversation, I'm privy to the conversation you're having with all these authors, saints, and sages, and I'm more aware of the internal conversation going on within me." I hope that as you read, you too will feel as if you are participating in a conversation on all levels: with the content, with me, and with your heart. As you read, I hope that you will imagine ways you might apply these practices in your current conversations and that you will create more occasions to explore your deepest yearnings, truths, and values in conversation with others.

Part One

What Is the Sacred Art of Conversation?

CONVERSATION AS A SACRED ART

Three-Dimensional Conversations

To "listen" another's soul into a condition of disclosure and discovery may be almost the greatest service that any human being ever performs for another.

—*Douglas Steere,*
Gleanings: A Random Harvest

At first glance, conversation appears to be a one-dimensional activity. It's a transaction where we give and receive information. In most introductory courses on communication, we are instructed to think carefully about what we want to say and how we want to say it, as everything we do communicates. The *how we say it* is as important, if not more, as the words we say. Listeners tend to focus much more on our nonverbal messages—our body language and tone of voice. As a student and teacher of communication studies, I knew that a whole lot more was going on in conversations than their verbal and nonverbal aspects.

I knew there were other dimensions in a conversation beyond the level of transaction because I had experienced them. There were moments when I felt as if I were being transported out of my own limited view of reality and into a deeper realm of mystery. I encountered truths about myself, others, and the divine Presence in our midst.

The renowned interviewer and oral historian Studs Terkel once described what happens in a conversation when it is really special. He told a story about a memorable conversation he shared with a woman, a mother of four little children, who had never before been interviewed. Their conversation was tape-recorded (a fairly new technology at the time). Terkel recalls:

> We finished the interview, and I feel kind of good. I got a hunch there's something here. I don't know what. I just feel kind of good. But the big thing is those kids, those five-, six-year-old kids jumping around the house. They want to hear mommy's voice. They know it plays back.... And so I'm playing back the voice that she herself never heard before. She never heard herself talking, or in this case, thinking as well as talking. And suddenly she said something on the microphone ... and she puts her hand to her mouth, "Oh, my God." And I said, "What?" And she says, "I never knew I felt that way before." Well, that's a great moment. She's saying, "I never knew I felt that way before." It's suddenly a discovery she's made as well as I'm making one. So it's as though we're both on a journey.[1]

Really special conversations offer occasions to disclose and discover our deepest thoughts and feelings. We experience mutual revelation: *It's suddenly a discovery she's made as well as I'm making one.* The meaning of revelation, from its Latin root *revelare*, is to lift the veil. Great conversations lift the veil, inviting us to discover more about ourselves, one another, and the sacred in our midst.

CHAPTER ONE

ENCOUNTERING THE SACRED WITHIN

There is a divine Abyss within us all, a holy Infinite Center, a Heart, a Life who speaks in us and through us to the world.

—*Thomas Kelly,* A Testament of Devotion

"All conversations are with myself, and sometimes they involve other people," observes Susan Scott in her book, *Fierce Conversations.*[1] Whether we are aware of it or not, we spend the majority of our time conversing with ourselves. Our capacity to be present in our external conversations depends upon our mindfulness of these internal conversations.

Our lives are filled with noise, and most of it is internal. We may resist getting really quiet, because we don't know what to do with all of this inner chatter. We tend to feel more anxious, not less, as our monkey minds jump from one thought to another. If we persist, we begin to discover a level of consciousness, a subtle awareness of an inner Presence, that we were not even aware we possessed. Perhaps that is why virtually every spiritual tradition that holds a vision of human transformation claims that cultivating a practice of intentional silence and stillness is imperative. Poet Jeannie E. Roberts describes her own experience of awakening to this inner Presence in the following excerpt from her poem, "The Pool":[2]

Beyond my flesh,
through jungles
of doubt
and despair,
down rivers
of restless dreams,
I slide
to waters
of perfect peace,
to a pool
divinely drenched
with light.
As I float
in the silence
that bathes my soul,
a stillness
fills my mind
with hope.
And I hear
an echo
from long ago,
an ancient voice
so clear, I know
beyond my flesh,
through jungles
of doubt
and despair,
down rivers
of restless dreams,

there's a pool
divinely borne,
where a voice
is waiting,
always waiting....

In order to discover this *pool divinely borne* within us, the Hebrew Scriptures implore us to "be still, and know that I am God!" (Psalm 46:10).

ENTERING THE CAVE OF YOUR HEART

> *If you had a temple in the secret spaces of your heart,*
> *what would you worship there?*
> —*Tom Barrett,* What's in the Temple

> *At the center of our being is a point of nothingness which is untouched by sin and illusion, a point of pure truth, a point or spark which belongs entirely to God.*
> —*Thomas Merton,* Conjectures of a Guilty Bystander

Have you ever heard yourself saying, "In my heart of hearts, I know that ..."? Being still, getting quiet, and listening within increases our attunement to the voice that dwells deep in our hearts. An array of faith traditions emphasizes the fundamental role of this inner sanctum. Hindu yogis refer to this interior place where the sacred dwells as *guha*—the cave of the heart.[3] The cave of the heart is a place deep within each of us known only to God. When we enter this cave in the depth of our hearts through various forms of prayer and meditation, we encounter the transcendent Mystery revealed in all of creation. This is not to suggest that the transcendent Mystery can be contained in our hearts; rather, this ineffable Mystery revealed in all of creation makes itself known in our hearts.

The more we practice entering the cave of our heart, the more we begin to notice that there is a conversation taking place deep within our heart. We may hear echoes of our heart's conversation in words another says that move us deeply or in a favorite song that we love to listen to over and over again. We may see a reflection of our heart's conversation as we gaze upon an object or a person that delights us, or we might be reminded of it as we observe an object or an event that disturbs us. Each of us has experiences that seem to whisper to us to pay attention to the conversation taking place deep within—to pause, to linger, and to listen deeply.

Throughout the past year, I've noticed that a large part of the conversation taking place in my heart is about my relationship with our son, Ryan. A young adult now, he began college in the fall. Although he applied for schools closer to home, some aspect of studying in Washington, DC, stirred his heart with enthusiasm. He departed with two very full suitcases in the middle of August, and I eagerly anticipated his first visit home during Thanksgiving break. Our week together was the first time in years that his dad and I had him all to ourselves—no classes or extracurriculars to attend and no job commitments. For a few brief days, we entered into a liminal space where we could focus on nothing but each other.

At the week's end, I found it even harder to say goodbye than when he had initially departed for college. When I returned home after dropping him off at the airport, I noticed a piece of popcorn on the garage doorstep. My natural tendency, as someone who likes tidiness and order, would have been to pick it up and toss it in the garbage can.

Yet, I noticed how seeing that piece of popcorn stirred some feeling deep within me, for I knew who had unintentionally dropped it there.

The popcorn has been there for six months now. I initially thought that I would pick it up and discard it after winter had passed. Instead, it has remained prominently displayed on the concrete step in our cold dark garage. Yes, the white popcorn did offer a bit of brightness in the midst of the bleak days of winter. But that's not why I left it there. That inconsequential piece of popcorn reminds me, each time I step out the door to leave or step into the door to return, of a long conversation taking place deep within my heart. Popcorn brings Ryan so much joy. Like his grandfather, if given the choice between a big bucket of movie theater popcorn and a full-course meal, the bucket of popcorn wins out every time. When I see that piece of popcorn, I often smile, even though I also feel an internal ache. That particular piece of popcorn is far more than a kernel to me. It reminds me to keep turning my attention to one of the prayers of my heart—that Ryan's life will be filled with joy.

Listen with the ear of your heart.

—*Saint Benedict,* Rule of Benedict

When we set aside a regular time, perhaps daily, to enter the cave of our heart and listen, we increase the likelihood that we will maintain awareness of the divine Presence within our hearts in the midst of daily activities. We cultivate our capacity to listen with the ear of our heart in our conversations with one another. As we become more mindful of the conversation in our own hearts, our joys, griefs, hopes, and concerns, we are more likely to be present to one another and less likely to project the themes of our internal conversations onto each other. We are more likely to speak the truth of our heart in our conversations with one another and to listen for the voice of the true self yearning to be revealed in one another's heart.

Practice: Entering the Cave of Your Heart

Each of us is invited to discover for ourselves where the cave of our heart is located within us. We learn to do this through repeated tuning in to the homing frequency at the depth of our being. The following heart meditation invites you to enter the cave of your heart, to rest there, and to begin to attune yourself to its subtle frequency.

> Adjust the position of your body.
>
> Sit up straight but relaxed by placing your feet on the floor, or by sitting on a cushion in a lotus or half-lotus position.
>
> Close your eyes completely or partially by looking toward the ground.
>
> Rest your hands gently in your lap.
>
> Begin breathing slowly and deeply.
>
> Observe your breath as it enters your nostrils and fills your diaphragm.
>
> Notice the sensation as your breath is released through your nostrils.
>
> As you breathe, you may notice that your body will begin to relax.
>
> However, your mind may continue to move rapidly.

In order to quiet and clear your mind, imagine a place deep within you that is filled with peace and stillness. As you continue to breathe deeply, gently turn your attention from your head to the cave of your heart. Continue to breathe in and out as you enter your heart and rest in its stillness and peace. If you find yourself distracted by thoughts, ever so gently return your focus to your breathing. Remain and rest there for as long as you wish.

When you are ready, open your eyes and bring this heart-filled awareness into your daily activities, especially your conversations with other persons.

Practice listening with the ear of your heart by reentering the cave of your heart throughout your conversations.

Practice: Listening to the Conversation in Your Heart

Each of us has experiences that beckon us to pay attention to the conversation taking place deep within—to pause, to linger, and to listen deeply. Over the course of the next day or week, take time to pause and listen to the conversation in your heart. Experiment with one or more of the following approaches as catalysts for evoking this inner conversation.

- Take a walk or sit quietly in a natural setting.
- Draw or paint a picture that captures the image(s) in your heart.
- Play one of your favorite songs or watch one of your favorite movies that speaks to your heart.

- Gaze upon an object or a person that delights you.
- Reflect upon an object or an event that disturbs you.

Rather than moving to the next activity, take some time to listen to the conversation in your heart at this moment in time:

- What are your heart's deepest yearnings?
- What is the prayer of your heart?
- What wisdom or guidance do you seek from your Inner Teacher?

CHAPTER TWO

ENCOUNTERING THE SACRED IN EACH OTHER

The wise see in every form the divine form; in every heart they see the divine light shining.

—Hazrat Inayat Khan,
The Complete Sayings of Hazrat Inayat Khan

Namaste. If I had to choose one word to capture the essence of the sacred art of conversation, it would be this Sanskrit greeting, which is often translated as "the divine in me greets the divine in you."

As we practice the sacred art of conversation, we are invited to increase our awareness of the divine in ourselves and in one another. Like the wooden Russian dolls whose whole being is not revealed by merely looking at their outermost layer, each of us contains additional layers within. These dolls symbolize a great spiritual truth. Truly encountering others involves seeing beyond the exterior and attending to one another's interior life. As we invite one another to open up and reveal our deeper layers, we discover a form that is at the very core of each one of us—our heart. In our heart, our intellect, will, and emotions are one and united. In our heart, we encounter divine wisdom—an Inner Light.[1] As we engage in a conversation, we are invited to tend one another's Inner Light, to encourage each other to keep paying attention to this source of truth in our hearts.

Although it was back in July, 1999, I remember the first week of my spiritual direction training experience as if it occurred yesterday. I had spent the majority of my adult life in school learning how to reason, deliberate, analyze, and assess. I now found myself seated in a circle with six other persons, and the only thing I was allowed to do was listen. As each trainee shared the story of his or her faith journey, no cross-talk—that is, back-and-forth discussion—was permitted. Moreover, after each of us had finished talking, we were not allowed to say anything in response to what we had just heard. It's not that there wasn't anything to say. From my perspective, there was plenty to say, plenty to ask, plenty of observations to share as other persons relayed their stories of experiences of joy and pain, clarity and confusion, consolation and desolation in their lives. I just couldn't figure out the point of all this listening if we could not respond to what we were hearing.

LEARNING A NEW WAY OF BEING PRESENT WITH ONE ANOTHER

> *Communication seems to take place sometimes without words having been spoken. In the silence we received an unexpected commission to bear in loving intentness the spiritual need of another person sitting nearby. And that person goes away, uplifted and refreshed.*
>
> —*Douglas Steere,* Quaker Spirituality

Learning the art of spiritual direction introduced me to an entirely different way of listening and being present in a conversation. Before training in the art of spiritual direction, my primary approach to engaging others in conversation was through active listening. In active listening, we paraphrase back to one another the thoughts and feelings we hear each other expressing. We then ask for confirmation. For example, "I heard you say that you're really fed up with your work. You feel frustrated. Your impression is you are undervalued. Is that what's going on for you? What more would you like to add?" When done well, active listening offers the potential to increase our understanding of one another. When done poorly, it's just one more technique we can use to really annoy each other. Training in the art of spiritual direction challenged me to go beyond adding more techniques to my repertoire. It invited me to enter into a fundamentally new way of participating in a conversation.

The Hebrew Scriptures remind us that "there is a time to keep silence, and a time to speak" (Ecclesiastes 3:7). Learning the art of spiritual direction underscored how imperative it is to keep silent and honor another's silence. Without a foundation of silence, it's hard to discern the source of our own and one another's words, to differentiate the voice of the Spirit from all the other voices clamoring for our attention. Cultivating silence may prove especially challenging for those of us who associate silence as a way of punishing one another or the inevitable silence in a conversation as an awkward moment to be avoided at all costs. We may find it hard to believe that sharing intentional silence can offer an experience to which we feel drawn. Quaker teacher Patricia Loring observes that silence is "not simply a running out of words, but is the fullness of awareness beyond words. It can become contemplation either of what is in the heart of the speaker or of the Loving Presence in which both are held."[2] Honoring the place of silence in our daily lives and in our conversation prepares us to attend to the deep stirrings within our own and one another's heart.

Listening deeply, and nothing more, can cultivate the virtue of restraint. Rather than trying to figure out the right thing to say as another is talking, we begin to learn how to keep the voice of our all-knowing egos in check. Our egos relish the opportunity to show how much we know, to demonstrate how effectively we can relate to and solve one another's problems, to try to be helpful. In sum, our egos like to pretend we are God—omniscient, omnipresent, and omnipotent. Until we begin to recognize the difference between the voice of our ego and the voice of the Spirit within us, we cannot be fully present to one another in a conversation. As we grow in our capacity to practice restraint, to differentiate the voice of our egos from the voice in our hearts, we no longer have to just listen. We can then respond with words, as it is more likely that our words will come from the core of our being, our heart. When they do, our words will typically be framed as questions or observations, rather than assertions. Our questions and observations have the potential to encourage others to listen to the wisdom waiting to be revealed in their hearts.

Encouraging One Another to Listen Within

> *God still lives and moves, works and guides, in vivid immediacy, within the hearts of men. For revelation is not static and complete, like a book, but dynamic and enlarging, as spring from a Life and Soul of all things.*
> —*Thomas Kelly,* Quaker Spirituality

We need each other's help to learn how to listen within. Since spiritual truth is often ineffable, we tend to find it difficult to put into words, to name, what it is we are hearing. In some cases, we need help gaining clarity about whether the voice we are hearing, which seems to be emerging from our heart, is in fact the voice of the Spirit—our Inner Teacher. At other times, we may be confident that the voice we are hearing is that of our Inner Teacher, yet remain unsure as to how to respond to what is being asked of us. And, truth be told, there are times when we know it is the voice of the Spirit speaking in our hearts, when we know how to respond to what is being asked of us, and yet resist doing so. For all these reasons, and more, it helps to have conversation partners to whom we can entrust our hearts, who can "listen" our souls into disclosure and discovery.

Reflection: Souls Who Have Made Us Wiser

We know in our heart of hearts when another person's words are echoing our inner truth and we also know when another person's words are violating it.

- Have you ever shared a conversation with someone whose soul made you feel wiser, someone who encouraged you to pay attention to the light within you, whose words seemed to echo your inner truth? Who was involved? What happened?
- What was it about that person's way of being that made your encounter so memorable and gratifying: for example, "I felt loved, respected, and accepted"; "I felt as if I had the other's undivided attention"; "I felt as if she was looking deep into my soul."
- Select one characteristic she or he exemplified, and set your intention to practice that way of being in a future conversation.

Practice: Tending One Another's Light—Holding, Beholding, and Being Held

Quakers teach us to reach out to the light of God within all persons. Through our conversations, we can invite one another to get in touch with the Light that is within each of us. The following ritual invites us to viscerally experience what it is like to hold, behold, and be held as we tend the Light Within. If this ritual is shared in a small group, it helps to have a facilitator who can ring a chime to signal each movement.

- Decide who will go first.
- Begin by lighting a tea light or small candle jar and hold it in your cupped hands. Sit quietly and notice how you feel as you *hold this light.*
- As you hold your light, invite your conversation partner to *behold the light* you carry without and within.
- When you are ready, invite your conversation partner to place his or her hands around yours. Notice what it feels like *to be held*, that is, to have another person contemplatively hold your light in his or her hands.
- Reverse roles.

The practice of holding our light, beholding one another's light, and having our light be held by each other offers an image for the sacred art of conversation.

CHAPTER THREE

ENCOUNTERING THE SACRED BETWEEN US

> *God is present when I confront You. But if I look away from You, I ignore him. As long as I merely experience or use you, I deny God. But when I encounter You I encounter him.*
>
> —*Martin Buber,* I and Thou

There once was a topsy-turvy town that had no roads and whose homes had no windows. The townspeople needed help. They believed that if they could find God, God would help them. Two of the townspeople, a woman and a man, were sent out in search of God. The woman climbed a tall mountain and set sail on a ship. The man traveled to the desert and listened for God in the dark quiet of a cave. Eventually, they each became tired and decided to stop looking for God. Yet, they both hoped that the other had found God:

> But when they met, the woman saw the man's drooping shoulders, and the man saw the woman's sad eyes. They knew that neither had found God. The woman put her cool hand on the man's sunburned arm, and the

> man wrapped his blanket around the woman. It was a dark moonless night, and [they] could see nothing but each other. In soft, small voices they talked long into the evening. They told each other their stories.

They returned to their town and helped each other put windows in every room of their homes, cut weeds, fill holes, and clear the rocks to build a road. The townspeople were stunned and sought an explanation. The man and woman replied that after journeying hundreds of miles to find God, they had found each other.

> "And we discovered God was with us," added the man.
>
> "With you? Right here?" puzzled the townspeople. "At home?"
>
> "Wherever we are," answered the woman....
>
> "But I can't see God anywhere," insisted one of the men of the town. "I just see you. If God is here, show us where."
>
> "God is in the between," said the man and the woman. "In the between. In between us."[1]

This story captures beautifully the way that transformation can occur when two or more people gather for conversation and share their stories with each other. This story helps introduce us to the ideas of one of the most important philosophers of the twentieth century, Martin Buber. Buber believed that we encounter the reality of God by meeting God in between—in our relationships with one another. Buber's philosophy provides some thoughts for us to consider as we try to practice the sacred art of conversation.

In his "philosophy of dialogue," Buber (1878–1965), an Austrian-born Jew, explores holiness in relationships, the potential for goodness in the individual, and the importance of the here and now. Buber believed that we find God by going out with our whole being to meet Thou—the sacredness within all beings. In his book, *I and Thou*, Buber proposed that there are two attitudes toward existence: I-It and I-Thou. In an *I-Thou* mode of relating, our intention is to *converse with* another in a fully personal manner. Buber believed that when we address another human being as someone made in the image and likeness of God, we encounter God. Conversely, in an *I-It* mode of relating, we speak to another in an impersonal manner as if she or he were an object. Because I treat you as less than human or don't recognize your full human dignity that reflects your being made in God's image, I ignore or deny God. Buber's understanding of relationships reminds us that every time we interact with another, we are offered an occasion to encounter the sacred. Buber calls our attention to a reality beyond the participants in a conversation that characterizes true dialogue—the realm of "between."[2]

Buber's invitation to encounter the realm of between can help us better understand distinctive characteristics of the sacred art of conversation:

- *To focus our intention on engaging with one another.* Conversation practiced as a sacred art is not a passive activity. In an I-Thou encounter, we participate in conversations by actively choosing to open our hearts to others. An I-Thou encounter requires self-awareness, a willingness to surrender control, and an investment of energy in getting to know another rather than a passive acceptance of someone else's definition of our partner in conversation. We can't sit back and resort to existing definitions, categories, or concepts to define the other. In the Gospel of John (4:1–26), Jesus encounters a Samaritan woman at a local well. Jesus might have chosen not to talk to her because of her marginal status as woman and as a foreigner. However, he intentionally defied the norms of his culture and society in order to reach out and engage her in a conversation.

- *To keep the focus on what goes on between us.* In the sacred art of conversation, we try to shift our focus from me, myself, and I to what's going on between us. Of course, our worries and responsibilities, our desire to make a good impression on others, our caution, and fears about expressing our deepest truth tend to keep us focused on ourselves and from opening up. Devoting time to self-reflection before and after our conversations increases the likelihood that we will maintain more of a focus on us throughout our conversation.
- *To keep our focus on the here and now by improvising.* Improvising requires us to focus our attention on the here and now—to what is happening in the moment. Rather than clinging to a preconceived idea of how a conversation should go, how another person should engage with us, how our relationship should unfold, we pay attention to what is unfolding in real time and respond accordingly.

Jazz musicians are the maestros of improvisation. One of my favorite examples of this capacity to improvise was a story

Herbie Hancock told about a lesson he learned in his early twenties from his great collaborator and mentor, Miles Davis. He described how he and Davis began their performance at a concert in Europe:

> We had the audience in the palm of our hands. And right as everything was really peaking, and Miles was soloing, I played this chord, and it was completely wrong. And Miles took a breath and then played some notes, and the notes made my chord right.... Somehow, what he chose to play fit my chords to the structure of the music.... What I learned from that is that Miles didn't hear the chord as being wrong. He just heard it as something new that happened. So, he didn't judge it. I learned the importance of being nonjudgmental, taking what happens and trying to make it work ... And it can lead you to other ideas, to something maybe you hadn't expressed before.[3]

In the sacred art of conversation, each of us discerns how to respond to the inevitable, though often unintentional, discordant chords that we and others play. When someone says something that conflicts with our values or offends us, what chord do we then play? Does another's discordant chord automatically hook us into playing a discordant chord of our own? Improvising requires us to focus our attention on the here and now—to what is happening in the moment. Rather than clinging to a preconceived idea of how a conversation should go, how another person should engage with us, how our relationship should unfold, we take what happens and try to make it work.

Reflection: Increasing Awareness of the Sacred Between Us

We can cultivate our capacity to honor the sacred between us by making a commitment to reflect upon the conversations we've shared, especially those that are significant to us.

- Was I willing to *look beyond appearances in order* to try to see your depth and uniqueness rather than looking at the role you occupy (e.g., neighbor) and the way I might categorize you (e.g., white male, blue collar, jock)?
- Was I willing to *focus on who you are in this moment and what you are talking about here and now* rather than being preoccupied with the things you've said in the past?
- Was I willing to focus *on what was emerging between us* rather than being overly concerned about your impression of me and what I was saying?
- Was I willing to *withhold judgment and improvise* when you said something that disturbed, disappointed, or defied my expectations?

Part Two

Gateways for Conversation

GATEWAYS FOR CONVERSATION

Following the Thread

May I live this day

Compassionate of heart,
Clear in word,
Gracious in awareness,
Courageous in thought,
Generous in love.
—*John O'Donohue,* To Bless the Space Between Us

There is a deep natural holiness waiting to be unlocked in our everyday encounters and relationships. By bringing more of our attention and a clearer sense of intention to our everyday interactions, our conversations can become for us a spiritual practice. Poet William Stafford offers a guiding metaphor to get us started:[1]

The Way It Is
There's a thread you follow. It goes among
things that change. But it doesn't change.
People wonder about what you are pursuing.
You have to explain about the thread.
But it is hard for others to see.
While you hold it you can't get lost.

Tragedies happen; people get hurt
Or die; and you suffer and get old.
Nothing you do can stop time's unfolding.
You don't ever let go of the thread.

Each of us has a thread that connects our life's tapestry. In some cases, others may wonder what we are following, as the thread is not always visible to them. Yet, let's face it. The thread is not always visible to us! We need each other's help to follow our thread. Our conversations with one another create occasions to reflect on the thread we have followed in our past, to notice the thread we are following in the present moment, and to discern where the thread we follow may be found in our future.

Through our conversations, we can learn more about the thread we have followed by listening to our life and sharing our stories with others. As we listen, we recognize the sacredness of our story, and with it, our emerging spiritual identity.[2] Really good conversation partners can help us discover that our stories don't have to have religious content in order to make them holy. Although we may find ourselves tempted to dismiss the messy, painful times as well as overlook our ordinary, routine activities as not having any spiritual significance, it is only by listening to our life, that is, by paying attention to all that has come our way, that we increase our awareness of the sacred thread running through our life's tapestry.

Through our conversations, we can learn more about the thread we are following in the present moment by carefully noticing our surroundings, our activities, our relationships, our interior thoughts and feelings. Really good conversation partners invite us to name what it is we are noticing, particularly in those moments that captivate our attention. By offering questions that invite one another to name what it is we find most sacred and life-giving in our daily lives, we can nurture one another's awareness and capacity for noticing even more.

Through our conversations, we can learn to discern where the thread we follow may be found in our future. Really good conversation partners encourage us to pause and reflect on our heart's stirrings, to pay attention to whether or not a path has heart for us. They listen, ask good questions, and encourage us to consider: Does the thought of following this path enliven rather than merely excite us? Will this path expand us, stretch us beyond our comfort zone, and invite us to grow? Does the thought of following this path increase our sense of connection with others and the world in which we live? Do the enthusiastic stirrings in our hearts persist even as we experience obstacles and setbacks?

In the following chapters, we will explore each of these three ways of unlocking the natural holiness in our conversations with one another.

CHAPTER FOUR

LISTENING TO YOUR LIFE

Surely the LORD is in this place—and I did not know it.

—Genesis 28:16

When I was a little girl, I would sit on my canopy bed and think about *the plan* for my life. I knew that someday, rather than playing school, I would be getting paid to teach. Someday, I would be married to a man as handsome as the one my Barbie doll hung out with (although his name wouldn't need to be Ken). And, perhaps, someday I might even have a child. We would live in Minnesota—in a house on a lake where I could spend a lot of time reading books. Between the canopy bed version of my life at age ten and the adult version, I imagined the in-between years of adolescence would be splendid. I'd be popular, have lots of friends, and continue to do very well in my classes.

The plan was clear and it gave me great comfort. I was a planner by nature and by nurture. When I was nine, my father sat my younger sister and me down at the kitchen table and coached us on how to write out our goals. In tandem, my mother's adage was and still is: "Don't leave things for the last minute; do as much as you can in advance; life goes more smoothly with advance preparation." If what happened in my life depended upon my capacity to reflect upon and articulate a plan, I had it all under control. I had done all the required preparation.

We all know what they say about the best-laid plans. For me, unlike the characters in Disney's "High School Musical" movies, high school was not the best time of my life. Instead, Fleetwood Mac offered the guiding maxim for my adolescent years: "Don't stop thinking about tomorrow.... Yesterday's gone, yesterday's gone." I was painfully aware that yesterday was gone—no more canopy bed, no more playing school, no more parents living together in the same house.

When I was eleven, my parents divorced. As a result, my mother moved my sisters and me from Minnesota to Phoenix, and the majority of my extended family now lived almost two thousand miles away. I no longer had the luxury of just being a child and focusing primarily on my own needs. Instead, my new life circumstances required me to be vigilant about my mother's loneliness and inevitable exhaustion, to find ways to maintain connection with my father and his new wife, to learn to accept our diminished socioeconomic status, and to try to adapt to a social environment that I never would have chosen for myself.

If someone had suggested to me then that God was at work in my life, I would have emphatically responded: I don't think so. God isn't in this place. I'll find God when I get back to *the plan*, get back to my home and extended family in Minnesota, get back to my Catholic school and my friends there, get back to the way things were, as that is the place where God is for me.

MAKING NEW MAPS FOR OUR JOURNEY

Each of us will inevitably encounter times in life that don't go according to *the plan*. Whether it's the breakup of a relationship or leaving our homeland, a diagnosis we've received or a loved one's illness we must endure, a period of long-term unemployment or the need to make a transition from a job that no longer fits us, we find ourselves in a wilderness, that is, a destination not of our own choosing.

Time in the wilderness is an archetypal theme found in the stories of various faith traditions. As we read the stories of the Hebrew people, Jesus, Muhammad, and the Buddha, we learn how wilderness times provide a catalyst for spiritual awakening. Such times invite us to increase our awareness of, and receptivity to, all that surrounds us, and perhaps, more important, all that resides within us. Although some of us may plan excursions into the wilderness, most of us are busy enough just trying to keep up with the demands of everyday life. It isn't until we find ourselves in what the poet John O'Donohue refers to as a "Genesis Foyer"—a key threshold or an unplanned wilderness experience in our lives—that we begin to pay attention within. O'Donohue offers the following counsel for when we find ourselves at such a threshold: "Take your time; Feel all the varieties of presence that accrue there; Listen inward with complete attention until you hear the inner voice calling you forward."[1] I find O'Donohue's eloquent words inspiring. Yet, let me confess. I don't like to take my time. I don't want to feel all the varieties of presences accruing in an experience, especially if they are painful. Even though I've gotten better at listening intently to the inner voice, I'm not always certain whether the voice I hear is the voice of God's Spirit beckoning me or my own very real need to just get on with it.

So, when all else fails, I have found that it really helps to have others to accompany me in the wilderness, those who encourage me to take my time and listen within, those who embody God's presence when God seems to be absent. In my faith tradition, Christianity, we refer to those who accompany us as spiritual companions, or *anamchara*, soul friends. Soul friends help us listen to our lives when we'd rather not or are unsure how to do so. Through their attentive presence, they invite us to pay attention to the sacred Mystery at work in our lives. As Margaret Wheatley observes:

> People who're lost in the mountains or wilderness, who either survive or die by the choices they make, at first fight to make their old maps work. They do everything possible to make the old maps fit the present circumstance—but they never can. In wilderness situations, this grasping goes on until the person is confronted with the fact that they're about to die. They will survive only if they acknowledge that there's no way out of their present peril; they must give up their old maps and acknowledge that they're truly lost. Once they recognize this, they begin to notice where they really are, what's going on, what's useful information available here and now. They make new maps and find their way home.[2]

Our soul friends encourage us to notice where we really are in order to make new maps and find our way home.

To make a new map, we need to pay attention to our life, listen to it, and let it speak its plan to us, implores educator and author Parker Palmer in his book, *Let Your Life Speak*:

> Before you tell your life what you intend to do with it, listen for what it intends to do with you. Before you tell your life what truths and values you have decided to live up to, let your life tell you what truths you embody, what values you represent.... I must listen to my life and try to understand what it is truly about—quite apart from what I would like it be about—or my life will

> never represent anything real in the world, no matter how earnest my intentions.[3]

When we cling too tightly to our old maps, *the plan* for our lives, we risk missing out on all the action taking place in the uncharted, expansive territory of our souls. Listening to our lives increases our receptivity to this deeper mystery at work.

Frederick Buechner emphasizes that "if I were called upon to state in a few words the essence of everything I was trying to say both as a novelist and as a preacher, it would be something like this: 'Listen to your life. See it for the fathomless mystery that it is. In the boredom and pain of it no less than in the excitement and gladness: touch, taste, smell your way to the holy and hidden heart of it because in the last analysis all moments are key moments, and life itself is grace.'"[4]

Listening to our life is not a one-shot deal. As many of us are learning, the most significant and complex experiences in our lives yield meaning over time. Buechner, now in his eighties, continues to try to make meaning of his father's suicide—an event that occurred more than seventy years ago. Through his numerous works of fiction and nonfiction, Buechner shows us that listening to our lives is not an exercise simply of sorting and assessing: "this was sacred, this was not." Rather, such listening invites us to pay attention for the sacred voice speaking at all times *to us* and at certain times *through us*, that is, increasing our receptivity to the still, small voice in the depths of our heart yearning to be heard. Buechner observes:

> The chances are we will never get it just right ... but if we keep our hearts and minds open as well as our ears, if we listen with patience and hope, if we remember at all deeply and honestly, then I think we come to recognize, beyond all doubt, that, however faintly we may hear

> him, he is indeed speaking to us, and that, however little we may understand of it, his word to each of us is both recoverable and precious beyond telling.[5]

Each time we listen to our life, we have the opportunity to discover, notice, and name more fully how God is at work. When we tell our stories in conversation with others, we create the occasion both to listen to our lives and to draw upon our life experiences as a source of truth. It is through listening to and sharing the stories of our life that we begin to make new maps for our journey.

Reflecting on Our Story

The capability to make meaning of our lives, and to tell our own distinctive story, begins to take shape in late adolescence and young adulthood. For those of us who are new to sharing the story of our journey, we may find it helpful to reflect upon the arc of our lived history as if we were preparing to write a book. We can begin by considering how we might respond to each of the following questions:

> If my life's journey were a book, I would title it ...
>
> The reasons I give my life this title are ...
>
> The chapters in the book of my life are ...
>
> The chapter I am in right now is ...
>
> I am currently discerning and trying to figure out ...
>
> As I imagine the next chapter on my journey, I hope ...

The first time we respond to these questions, or invite others to do so, we may find that our responses are fairly brief. We might only be able to respond to each question in a sentence or in a few words. However, the more we commit to listening to our life and composing our story through journaling or conversation with others, we find that our short responses begin to lengthen.

As we share our stories, we need not be overly concerned about narrating *the entirety* of our life's experiences, even if it were possible to do so. Realistically, if each of our lives were a feature film, much of its contents would end up on the cutting room floor.[6] Certain features of our lived experience prove salient to us; others do not. Even if two people were to live the exact same set of events, the experience of such events would result in different narratives.[7] We find that the more we reflect upon our lived experience, the more we recognize that *there is more than one way to tell our story*.

Through the telling of our stories, our awareness of alternative, richer narratives increases. For example, earlier in my life, I might have called the chapter in my life when my parents divorced "Broken Apart." I was consumed then with loss and grief and felt a lack of control over the events that had occurred. My narrative tended to focus on fault-finding and contained many *if onlys*: *if only* my father had been faithful to my mother; *if only* we had stayed in Minnesota; *if only* my parents had reunited, I would be whole again. As I look back today at the same set of events, I now interpret and name this chapter "Breaking Open."

Perhaps the most significant aspect of listening to others' stories and sharing our own is the realization that our stories are not set in stone. In listening to and composing our lives, we abandon the notion of the past as having a meaning and work to extract alternative meanings that may prove more life-giving. God's action in our lives is always open to new interpretation.

Through their genuine curiosity, commitment, and alertness to our verbal and nonverbal communication, really good conversation partners help us notice aspects of our stories that have particular energy for us. They ask us meaningful questions that invite us to step back from the action and to reflect on our wishes, motivations, values, and beliefs.[8] They encourage us to not settle for thin narratives, to continue to listen for the enigmatic expression of the Spirit whose meaning isn't readily apparent and continues to be revealed over time. In considering others' questions and observations, we can't help but examine our stories in new ways.

Letting Our Life Speak Through Storytelling

We need to create more occasions for listening to our lives and letting our lives speak, for people typically don't tell their story in much detail unless they are asked to do so and an occasion for doing so is created. Psychologist Ira Progroff, who developed a comprehensive process designed to help people discover and deepen their understanding of their lives through journaling, observes: "In the lives of many persons the quest for meaning is left implicit and unarticulated.... While the questions and wonderings are there, the circumstances of outer life in most societies tend to discourage people from giving outer expression to inward sensitivities and to private intimations of truth."[9]

In 2003 Dave Isay set up a recording booth in New York's Grand Central Terminal where forty-minute interviews were conducted between family members and friends. Isay believes that each of us has a valuable story to tell. His StoryCorps Project is based upon a few ideas: "That our stories—the stories of everyday people—are as interesting and important as the celebrity stories we're bombarded with by the media every minute of the day. That if we take the time to listen, we'll find wisdom, wonder, and poetry in the lives and stories of the people all around us. That we all want to know our lives have mattered and we won't ever be forgotten. That listening is an act of love."[10]

Listening is an act of love. As we listen to another's story, our role is not to interpret the meaning of how God is at work in another's life. Rather, we strive to listen for the sacred currents *beneath* the stream of the person's life. As listeners, our intent is not to challenge a narrative but to invite the teller to dig deeper, to unpack it, to thicken it, to offer the possibility of considering it from a different perspective.[11]

Our stories—the ones we tell and those we are told—shape us. Each of us is a story catcher, or more accurately, a story sponge, absorbing stories from many different sources (our family, culture, faith traditions, and the media, among others). It's not what's happened in our past that defines us, but the stories we attach to the past. For example, there are many adults like me whose parents divorced when they were children. Some of us may tell a story about being the victim of such an event, for example, how their parents' divorce debilitated them and kept them from ever experiencing true intimacy with others. Others may tell a more redemptive story recounting how their resilience increased as a result of the disintegration of their family.

Perhaps the most important response that we as conversation partners can offer one another is the encouragement to practice what narrative therapists refer to as "relentless optimism," the recognition that "God is constantly at work in our personal and collective stories to realize God's dream for us. Although we may not pay attention to this ongoing work, it's there nonetheless—God's persistent, compassionate presence ... is always at work to offer an alternative narrative."[12]

Gathering with one another to practice relentless optimism and help each other notice and name the particularities of our lived experience nurtures our awareness of how *God was in this place even when we did not know it.*

Reflection: Steppingstones on the Journey

Begin by journaling your responses to one or more of the guiding reflection questions. Bring one or more of the following questions into a future conversation and invite others to respond:

- At this time in my journey, I am ...
- As I take the next step on my journey, I hope ...
- As I take the next step on my journey, I seek ...
- As I take the next step on my journey, I wonder ...
- As I take the next step on my journey, I fear ...
- What I have learned from earlier steps I have taken on my journey is ...
- As I take this next step, I want to remember ...

CHAPTER FIVE

NOTICING AND NAMING WHAT GIVES YOU LIFE

I write for other people with the hope that I can help them to see the wonderful things within their everyday experiences. In short, I want to show people how interesting the ordinary world can be if you pay attention.

—Ted Kooser

My eyes filled with tears as I listened to Jeffrey Brown interview Ted Kooser on the "PBS NewsHour." Kooser had just been named the thirteenth National Poet Laureate of the United States. I was fascinated by Kooser's humble, calm, and unassuming demeanor as he spoke: "In my work, I really try to look at ordinary things quite closely to see if there isn't a little bit of something special about them."[1] As an adolescent, he knew he wanted to write poetry and yet also recognized that it would be difficult to make a living as a poet. Therefore, for most of his adult life, he wrote poetry for an hour or two before spending a full day at the office as an insurance executive. He reflected: "I never saw myself as an insurance executive, but

rather as a writer in need of a paying job." In an effort to make his poetry accessible to as many readers as possible, he would regularly show the poems he was working on to his secretary. If she didn't get them, he'd make changes.

In the interview Kooser also talked about being diagnosed with cancer. After his diagnosis, he retired from his insurance work and didn't do any writing while undergoing radiation. He resumed writing after his treatment ended and began walking a couple of miles every morning. Following each morning walk, he wrote a short poem about what he had seen that particular day: "It was very important for me to see something from each day that I could do something with and find some order in, because I was surrounded by medical chaos or health chaos of some kind." He pasted his daily poem on a postcard and sent it to a friend. Over the course of a winter, he wrote and shared 130 short poems.[2]

Kooser believes that each of us is invited to practice this discipline of noticing in our daily lives. In his book, *The Poetry Home Repair Manual: Practical Advice for Beginning Poets*, Kooser describes his writing process: "When something happens to catch your attention, and you feel like making a note of it, you can usually trust your impulse. There may well be something there worth writing about. Chances are good that you've noticed whatever it is because somewhere within you, you have a glimmer of feeling about it. At first you may not recognize or be able to elucidate that emotion, but as you work with your words the feelings can be expected to come forward."[3]

Kooser had named for me, and underscored, some essential lessons of the spiritual life: *Look closely. Notice what moves you and evokes a glimmer of feeling. Put it into words. Share what you are noticing with others.* So, rather than saying to myself, oh, what an interesting interview I just saw on the "NewsHour" and getting on with my day, I followed Kooser's lead. I took some time to explore and put into words: Why is this interview moving me to tears? What is this glimmer of feeling about?

In my first attempt to name what I was noticing, I thought: Ted Kooser's story gives me hope. At the time I watched his interview, in October 2004, I was in the midst of a difficult professional transition. I was feeling stuck in my academic career and often lamented that *if only* I had attended a more impressive institution or specialized in a different discipline, I wouldn't be in the predicament I was in. I just loved the fact that Kooser didn't seem concerned about pedigree or being anyone other than who he was. He celebrated the particularity of his life by writing about the places he knows best. He didn't say to himself: if only I lived on the West Coast, then I could be a poet and write about the beauty of the mountains or the ocean. Instead, abiding in the plains of Nebraska, his poetry focuses on what he finds remarkable about the Bohemian Alps (as he endearingly refers to his native landscape).[4] His story offered me a much needed reminder: "Focus on where you are, who you are, and the particularities of your life rather than striving to be or get somewhere else."

As I reflected further, I noticed that his way of being delighted my heart. Kooser's commitment to *helping others see the wonderful things within their everyday experiences and showing people how interesting the ordinary world can be if you pay attention* resonated with my own. Moreover, he practiced what he preached. I was enamored not only with his decision to notice something on each daily walk, but also that he took the time to name it and share it with others by writing a poem and mailing it to a friend. This level of intentionality in daily life, in the midst of illness and adversity, was not only striking. It was inspiring.

INCREASING OUR CAPACITY TO NOTICE

I recently read that the mind without spiritual training can only focus on anything or anyone for no more than two minutes.

This involuntary form of attention has its advantages. We aren't likely to miss the honking car in our path or the person who yells to get out of the way. However, given that many of us are bombarded by new sounds and screens galore, most of us are chronically overstimulated. We suffer from perpetual distraction and maintain continuous partial attention as we move through our days. We tend to see the neon lights but often miss the subtle beauty of candlelight; we tend to hear the cell phone ringing but may miss the sadness in the tone of a friend's voice; we revel at the ocean waves on our vacation but miss the grandeur of the changing leaves in our back yard. And, yet, we do have another choice.

In 1994, feeling "increasingly dissatisfied" with his art, renowned photographer Jim Brandenburg undertook a personal project. He challenged himself to take only one photograph per day for ninety days. If you aren't familiar with Brandenburg's work, you may ask: so what's the big deal? Anyone can take a picture a day. Well, here's the backstory: Prior to this, in his more than twenty-five-year tenure with *National Geographic*, Brandenburg had traveled the world taking pictures. For each project, he often shot up to three hundred rolls of film only to have a few dozen photos selected for a published article. For him, it is an understatement to suggest that taking only a single picture a day was an act of creative restraint. After the shutter of his camera opened and closed on that first autumn day, his journey commenced.

By watching the documentary film *Chased by the Light*, about this ninety-day project, you begin to see the world through Brandenburg's eyes.[5] As he traipses about the Northern Minnesota landscape discerning which image to capture each day, he doesn't seem anxious about whether or not he'll find objects or people or events worth photographing nor overwhelmed at the prospect of limiting his choice to just one image. In short, he doesn't seem concerned about the outcome; rather, he waits with expectancy, receptivity, and patience.

Brandenburg's self-imposed ninety-day project was an exercise in learning to notice. Artists like Brandenburg remind us that seeing involves more than just looking at someone or something.[6] They show us that in order to really see, to notice, we must get ourselves out of the way. That is, we must learn to open our eyes and be willing to sacrifice what we would like to happen, our agenda, and be receptive to what is actually happening. With saints and sages, artists learn to surrender their I-hood and try to see "things for their sake, not for your own."[7] In order to see things as they are, they encourage us to be still, wait patiently, and watch closely. Whether it's a matter of deciding which image to capture in a photograph or how to respond to another who seems unwilling to talk, developing our capacity to see is not so much a way of seeing as it is a way of being, and for most of us it is a gradual one.

Novelist Ann Patchett describes a lesson she continues to learn: "To pay attention to the things I'll probably never need to know, to listen carefully to the people who look as if they have nothing to teach me, to see school as something that goes on everywhere, all the time, not just in libraries but in parking lots, in airports, in trees."[8] She shared this lesson and others in her commencement address for the graduates of her alma mater, Sarah Lawrence College. In her talk, titled "What Now?," she described how learning to pay attention had prepared her for her work as a writer. She reflected that she didn't fully become a writer until she worked as a dishwasher at T.G.I. Friday's. As she washed, she learned to stare, be still, get quiet, and think things through. In the end, she believes it was her learning to stare that enabled her to develop as a novelist.

Whether it's writing a daily poem, taking a single picture, or observing one's internal thoughts while washing dishes, all are ways of cultivating intentional attention. The reason poets like Kooser, photographers like Brandenburg, and authors like Patchett are so good at noticing is that they practice noticing on a daily basis. Moreover, by naming what it is they are noticing through writing a poem, taking a picture, or creating a story, these artists nurture both their own and our awareness. They open our eyes to new ways of seeing familiar activities and encourage us to look more deeply at that which is unfamiliar or uncomfortable.

The more we look closely and focus our full attention on our surroundings, our activities, our relationships, and our interior thoughts and feelings, the more we tend to notice. Like these artists, each of us has the opportunity to name what it is we are noticing through journaling or in conversations with others. In so doing, we nurture our own awareness and capacity for noticing even more, and we have the potential for nurturing others' awareness. Eventually, noticing becomes a way of life.

NOTICING AS A WAY OF PRAYING

> *It is wisely said, "Experience is the best teacher...." The primary and most obvious reason for this is that revelation is not over, God is constantly revealing himself to us in our experience.... Of course, the Bible is divine revelation—no one denies that. But so is life! It is precisely because God is present to life and available to human experience that we have a divinely inspired story to tell, and that the story told is revelation.*
>
> —*Dick Westley,* A Theology of Presence

I used to think of prayer as an activity, that is, something to do each day. Ideally, prayer was an activity I was supposed to do first thing in the morning. On days that I didn't make the time for prayer, I often felt guilt-ridden the rest of the day. However, the more I practiced noticing, the more I began to see that prayer can be a way of life.

Praying is a form of attention. Concentrating our attention has the potential to bring more light into our souls, claimed Simone Weil.[9] Attention was one of the central themes of Weil's spirituality, and, for her, the essence of all prayer. Weil defined prayer as the orientation of all the attention of which the soul is capable toward God. In her own short life, she cultivated her capacity for attention through her work as a philosopher, teacher, activist, and author. For Weil, religion is nothing else but looking and prayer nothing more than turning toward God, the desire and receptivity of "waiting for God." In this way of praying there are no methods to remember or techniques to learn. She believed that we are praying whenever we turn our full attention to the presence of God. We are praying whenever we suspend ourselves as the center of the world and make ourselves available to the reality of another being—be it God or neighbor.

By beginning our days in intentional quiet, pausing throughout the day to listen within, and ending our day in quiet reflection, we can increase our attentiveness to God's presence. More than five hundred years ago, Saint Ignatius of Loyola developed a spiritual exercise for increasing attentiveness to God's presence that he called the "examen." Ignatius encouraged his followers to devote time each day to reflecting upon their activities, including the places, persons, and tasks, and noticing the feelings that surfaced, both positive and negative, in the midst of the action by considering: When did I feel most alive today? When did I feel life draining out of me?[10]

Ignatius believed that God's revelation is ongoing and that God speaks through our deepest feelings and yearnings. The most sacred aspects of our lives are those that are life-giving, not life-denying. When we experience abiding joy and peace, it's usually an indication of sacred attunement. In addition to reflecting upon what we have noticed in a given day, we can practice the examen as a way of noticing and reflecting upon any significant experience (a conversation, a poem or sacred scripture passage, a movie, a book) or a period of time (a week, a year, or on special occasions such as holidays, birthdays, and anniversaries).[11]

NOTICING IN CONVERSATION

Learning to notice is a sacred invitation. In his book, *Spiritual Mentoring*, Tad Dunne reminds us that noticing is fundamental to being human:

> Before any knowledge of God came questions about God. Before any questions came noticing. Before noticing came a dark and relentless desire. It can come as a shock to realize this essential role of human noticing, questions, and desire in divine revelation. But it is a healthy shock. We discover a profound camaraderie with all the men and women who seek the truth about life. We are engaged in the same struggle they are. What they discovered about God they pass on to us, not as mere information but as an invitation to notice, to wonder, to question, and to realize for ourselves.[12]

The more we take the time to look closely, to pay attention to what glimmers and moves us deeply, and to try to put into words what we are noticing, the more our awareness of the sacredness of everyday life will be nurtured.

We extend this invitation in our conversation with others whenever we move from asking conventional questions to offering questions that invite others to notice, name, and nurture their awareness of what they find to be life-giving. Instead of asking the next person we meet, "What do you do for a living?" we might try, "Where are you finding joy in your life these days?" Instead of asking a child, "How do you like school?" we might try, "What's the best part of being a fourth grader?" Instead of asking our coworker, "What can be done to improve the morale in our office?" we might ask instead, "What do you enjoy most about your work?" Through this commitment to noticing and naming what we hold sacred, and inviting others to do the same, we increase our collective awareness of the sacred in our midst. We grow to see more of the truth, beauty, and goodness in our daily lives—"to look at ordinary things quite closely to see if there isn't a little bit of something special about them."

Reflection: Nurturing Awareness of What You Hold Sacred

What captures our attention in the outer world invites us to get in touch with the hidden treasure within us. We can cultivate the habit of paying attention. The following questions can be used for personal reflection or shared in a conversation.

- *Notice.* As you reflect upon your experiences from this day (or this week), what experience seems to shimmer and connect with a glimmer of feeling?
- *Name.* Describe the experience. Try to put into words what you are noticing by reflecting: what is this experience about for me at this time in my life?
- *Nurture.* Share what you have noticed and named. Write about it in a journal. Tell a friend about it in

conversation. Invite other persons to tell you about an experience that is shimmering for them.

Reflection: Looking at the World with the Eyes of a Poet

The following exercise is taken from John Fox's book, *Poetic Medicine: The Healing Art of Poem-Making.*[13] It invites you to reflect upon what touches and moves you deeply at this time in your life. Begin by writing a response to one or more of the following sentence stems. If you find yourself drawn to one question in particular, feel free to stay with it and see where it takes you. After you've had time to reflect, consider asking one or more of these questions in a future conversation.

- What I long to see healed in my world is ____________.
- The beauty of ______________________ is a source of joy in my life.
- The neglect of _____________________ makes me sad.
- I am determined to change the treatment of ___________________________ in this world.
- My heart is broken open by the loss of ___________________________ in this world.
- My creative spirit is kept alive by people who express the following: _________________________________.

CHAPTER SIX

DISCERNING A HEART-CENTERED PATH

It is only with the heart that one can see rightly.
What is essential is invisible to the eye.
—*Antoine de Saint-Exupéry,* The Little Prince

It was the beginning of the Lenten season and a flyer advertising an upcoming retreat caught my attention. I'm typically game for a good retreat. Yet, as I read the description, I was puzzled. This was a doll-making retreat. Since I feel inept at artsy-crafty activities, I threw the information away. A couple of days later, my dear friend, Lucy, called and asked if I would be interested in attending the retreat with her. Since Lucy is a gifted visual artist, I knew this doll-making stuff would be right up her alley. I told her of my ambivalence about attending. Yet, since I had recently asked her to attend an event that initially made her feel uncomfortable, it seemed the least I could do was reciprocate the risk-taking and stretch outside my comfort zone.

As Lucy and I entered the room the morning of the retreat, we found tables filled with fabrics and sequins and supplies galore. There was a buzz in the room. As the retreat leader displayed some of the dolls that she or others had made on previous retreats, there were oohs and ahhs and a giddy anticipation about what the day would hold. As I looked at those dolls, I thought: I don't get this. What's the point? I found myself fantasizing about pulling a ripcord and landing in a meditation room filled with zafus—a day devoted to doing nothing more than sitting and watching the breath. Nonetheless, I was intrigued as I listened to the retreat leader describe the guiding principle for designing a doll: listen within at each step in the process and let your inner guide shape your unfolding creation.

We began by taking a small amount of wet clay to mold the doll's head. As the clay started drying and cracking, I was dismayed. The face seemed so ugly. I wondered: what on earth is my inner guide trying to convey? The next step was to choose the doll's hair. Since that just seemed like too much work, I decided (I'm not sure whether or not my inner guide had anything to do with it) that my doll was going to be bald. Then again, it must have been my inner guide because a girly girl like me would never choose baldness over long hair and curls. And it was at that point that I knew that my doll wanted to be a man.

After the head and hair were complete, we then attached the doll's head to a bottle that served as its body. It was then time to paint the face. We were instructed to begin with the eyes. However, as I began to paint the color around the pupil of the first eye, the paint smeared. So I had a choice: I could try to compensate for my error, cover it with white paint, and start again, or I could go with it. In a spirit of cooperation with my inner guide and what I might discover about myself from my seeming error, I went with it. As the paint dried, the eyes took on a cloudy, milky appearance—like the eyes of someone who could not see. So now my doll was not only bald, he was also blind.

The next to last step was to choose the doll's clothing. Okay, I must admit, I enjoyed that part. Since I really like matching and coordinating colors, I chose fabric that would match with my home—especially the sage color in my living room. I noticed that this particular color was very compelling to me. Since I prefer fairly simplistic dressing with little to no emphasis on accessories, I found myself surprised by how drawn I was to a large warm red heart on the table. Somehow I just knew that this heart was the only accessory my bald and blind doll needed. However, I found that placing the large warm red heart over the doll's sage fabric robe had a garish and disturbing effect. Instead, I nestled it underneath his garment; his large heart did not need to be visible to others.

The final step was to discern a name for my doll. We left the room with all the doll-making materials and were invited into a candlelit space where the retreat facilitator guided us through an imagery exercise. We were to listen deeply within for what our doll wanted to be named. This last step proved to be the easiest for me. His name emerged clearly: Trailblazer. I felt emboldened to give my doll this name as I recognized that this doll had a remarkable gift: he no longer had to depend on his outer senses to find his way in the world. His quest was to live from his heart and to see the world with the eyes of his heart.

I learned a great deal from my doll-making retreat experience. As John O'Donohue observes in his book *Beauty: The Invisible Embrace*:

> The imagination offers revelation. It never blasts us with information or numbs us with description. It coaxes us into a new situation. As the scene unfolds, we find ourselves engaged in its questions and possibilities, and new revelation dawns. Such revelation is never a one-off

> hit at the mind. The knowing is always emerging. The imaginative form of knowing is graced with gradualness.[1]

Clearly, this retreat had coaxed me into a new situation. Throughout the day I learned much more about my attachments and my aversions. I'm attached to a certain conception of beauty, averse to anything that appears ugly; attached to order, averse to chaos; attached to being in control and knowing where things are going, averse to surprises and risk-taking. Although I was well aware of these attachments and aversions prior to the retreat, I suspect my feelings of resistance throughout the day had to do with the inevitability of being reminded of them. A new form of knowing had emerged gradually throughout the day. Trailblazer reminded me that I had to look beyond appearances. In order to see, I had to open the eyes of my heart.

Our Heart's Inner Compass

> *The heart is the center of our being and our most comprehensive cognitive faculty. The eye of the heart sees more truly than our ego-based intellect and emotions. With such a heart, true surrender, and true happiness and well-being, become possible.*
>
> —*Kabir Helminski,* The Knowing Heart

"Follow your heart. It knows the way" is embroidered on a pillow that rests on my office chair. I like to sprinkle my environment with reminders of wisdom sayings I want to make sure I don't forget. I bought this particular pillow two years ago. It reflects my growing commitment to follow my heart. However, this whole business of learning to follow our heart is easier said than done.

Each of us possesses an inner compass. In order for us to activate it, author Margaret Silf reminds us:

> We must come to stillness. In the silence of our hearts, we must wait patiently for the compass needle to steady. Then it will point to true north, the still center, the fine point of the soul, and we will be enabled to move forward again.[2]

Whether we're deciding what to do next as we design an artistic creation or discerning what gives our life purpose and meaning, we need to *listen within and let the inner compass of our heart provide direction*.

In Paulo Coelho's beloved book, *The Alchemist*, a shepherd boy named Santiago sets out in search of a treasure. Over the course of his journey, Santiago learns the importance of listening to his heart in order to discover his treasure. Those whom he meets on his journey remind him that there is a language in the world that everyone understands. It is the language of enthusiasm. As he encounters obstacles and adversity on his quest, Santiago discerns the next step on his path by continuing to pay attention to the stirrings of enthusiasm in his heart.

Yaqui Indian Don Juan echoes this guiding principle of paying attention to your heart. He advised the anthropologist Carlos Castaneda to look at every path closely and deliberately and then ask himself one question: "Does this path have a heart?" If it does, the path is good. If it doesn't, it is of no use. Buddhist Jack Kornfield unpacks this principle:

> When we ask, "Am I following a path with heart?" we discover that no one can define for us exactly what our path should be. Instead, we must allow the mystery and beauty of this question to resonate within our being. Then somewhere within us an answer will come and

> understanding will arise. If we are still and listen deeply, even for a moment, we will know if we are following a path with heart.... We can actually converse with our heart as if it were a good friend.[3]

PAYING ATTENTION TO OUR HEART'S STIRRINGS

The heart is the one center that connects us on the religious level with all human beings. In recognition of the crucial role the heart played, the Hebrew people prayed: "Create in me a clean heart, O God, and put a new and right spirit within me" (Psalm 51:10). By taking time each day to pause and reflect upon the conversation in our heart, we cultivate the habit of discernment in our daily lives.

Discernment (from the Latin *discernere*) means to separate, distinguish, determine, and sort out. In discernment we are invited to attend to our feelings, our thoughts, and our desires. Discernment is "sifting through" our inner and outer experiences to determine their origin—whether they are the voice of our ego (our limited self) or the Spirit. Imam Jamal Rahman underscores that as we pay attention to the conversation in our hearts our capacity to distinguish the voice of our ego from that of our real guide increases:

> Become silent, go within, and listen. By reflecting in this way again and again, the wise teacher within begins to emerge. Initially, you might hear several voices in you. If you listen to the voice of the ego and make a mistake, be compassionate with yourself and persist. With practice you learn discernment and eventually connect with the voice of your real guide.[4]

Discerning a path with heart requires commitment and discipline. The practice of discernment is not a one-shot deal or a strategy to pull out of our toolkit only on those occasions when we are faced with big decisions (e.g., Should I take job *a* or *b*? Should I marry now or wait until I'm done with school? Should I retire or try to find a different type of work?). Ideally, discernment becomes a way of life as we cultivate the daily habit of pausing and reflecting on our heart's stirrings.

DISCERNING A PATH WITH HEART IN CONVERSATION

> *Do you have the patience to wait till your mud settles and the water is clear? Can you remain unmoving till the right action arises by itself?*
>
> —*Lao-Tzu,* Tao Te Ching

It's hard enough to try to discern and follow one's own path with heart, let alone accompany others as they discern and follow theirs. Yet, I find that the more I practice pausing and listening each day to what is stirring within my heart, the better prepared I am to listen to others. Our most helpful conversation partners invite us to talk about the paths we are considering. At times, we may experience revelation, a holy aha, as we listen to ourselves tell others about a situation we are discerning. As we do so, the way becomes clear. At other times, we seek greater clarity about the next best step to take. During these times, others' questions prove particularly helpful as they invite us to listen within for the guidance of our Inner Teacher. During those inevitable times in our lives when no path seems clear, our most helpful conversation partners encourage us to trust and wait "for the mud to settle and the water to clear" rather than make a hasty, impulsive decision.

As we discern in a conversation whether or not a path has heart for us, *it helps to begin by pausing and inviting one another to pay attention to whether the thought of a particular path stirs and moves us deeply*. If we imagine undertaking an activity and it bring tears to our eyes along with a sense of overwhelming joy and enthusiasm, that's a good sign. I remember having that feeling when I visited one of my son's schools for the first time. I was so moved by the place, and the energy of the people within it, that I wanted to go to school there. Conversely, when something starts clanging within us, similar to a five-alarm fire in our gut, then whatever we are considering is not a path with heart. For example, you receive a job offer. All the conditions seem right: it pays well, it's a good fit for your skills, and the people with whom you will be working are great. Yet, you don't feel enthusiastic about the prospect. Something seems to be missing, even though you're not quite sure what it is. You feel hesitant about saying yes. You don't feel a deep sense of peace about doing so. These are usually indicators that this path is not for you. If you can, delay the decision for a time, and return to it again. When feelings of uncertainty persist, we need to encourage one another to keep paying attention. Although this may be a good path, based upon appearances, another path may prove to be the better choice.

Although the experience of a desire stirring deep within us is a starting point for our discernment, the process doesn't end there. I feel stirred and moved to tears by watching Hallmark movies. Sometimes what stirs us may be a reflection of our conditioning. Therefore, we need to invite one another to reflect upon the following questions.

Does the thought of following this path truly enliven rather than merely excite us? All too often we may only pay attention to whether a prospect excites us. However, our egos find many aspects of life exciting. It sounds exciting to me to go on a shopping spree at my favorite clothing store. Yet it is important to distinguish between what excites us and what enlivens us.

What excites us often passes. What enlivens us tends to endure. Going on a shopping spree may be great fun at the time, I'm sure of it, yet I know I wouldn't feel enlivened when I received the bill. Conversely, the prospect of spending a year or more writing a book is not terribly exciting. You work in isolation and you have to say no to a lot of other things in order to get it done. Yet, however unexciting writing a book may be at times, I find it an incredibly enlivening path even on those days when the writing goes slowly and I don't accomplish much.

Does the path we are considering taking expand us, stretch us beyond our comfort zone, and invite us to grow? Although a shopping spree would definitely expand the contents of my closet, writing expands my sense of self and what I aspire to contribute to others. We can be pretty confident that a path has heart for us if we foresee that it will challenge and stimulate us. If an activity or a relationship invites us to be more than we think we can be, offers more than we believe we are capable of offering, increases our hope, kindles our imagination, and offer us a sense of possibility, however small, we should see these as promising signs that we should take the next step.

As we continue to discern with one another whether a stirring is emanating from the depth of our heart or the surface of our ego, we encourage one another to *pay attention to whether following a path increases our sense of connection with others and the world in which we live*. Following a path with heart invites and challenges each of us to strike a fine balance between inward listening to our hearts and outward, socially engaged listening with our hearts to the realities of the world in which we live.[5] If the path I am considering taking seems to benefit only me, and not my family or community, then it's probably all about me. If a path truly has heart, it will enhance real communion and benefit others in our community and beyond.

Do the enthusiastic stirrings in our hearts persist even as we experience obstacles and setbacks? Perhaps the ultimate test is whether the path we are considering taking continues to appeal to us even if the prospect of following it doesn't prove to be easy. At times, we may discern that to take this job or to volunteer for this project or to begin this relationship isn't logical. We can't grasp how we could make it work given all the other commitments in our lives. However, if you find yourself continuing to think about a path, and feeling stirred by it, and beginning to imagine how it could possibly work, it may indeed be a path that has heart for you. If you continue to feel drawn to it, keep paying attention. If you find yourself feeling driven to pursue it—for example, you are feeling anxious, worrying, hurrying, and trying to make things happen—then it's most likely your ego trying to run the show rather than your heart resonating with a path.

Rather than give us advice as to which path they think we should follow, our most helpful conversation partners invite us to keep paying attention to whether or not a given path resonates with our heart's stirrings. They also help us remember. They remind us of the values, hopes, and dreams that we talked about in the past but may have otherwise forgotten or overlooked. And, on those occasions when we resist taking a step onto a heart-centered path, they invite us to explore what might be learned from encountering our resistance.

Reflection: Listening to Your Inner Guide

- Does the prospect of following this path fill your heart with joy and enthusiasm?
- Does this path truly enliven rather than merely excite you?

- Does this path expand your heart—that is, increase your capacity to love and care and reach out to others?
- Does this path strengthen your sense of connection with your truest self, others, and the world in which you live?
- What thoughts, feelings, or images persist and recur as you consider following this path?
- Based upon the information you have identified, what is the next best step you can take at this time?

Reflection: The Thread You Follow

- What is the thread you are following?
- At what point in your life did you become consciously aware that you were following a thread (e.g., a divine thread, a thread of meaning and purpose, a calling)?
- Have other people ever wondered about what you are pursuing? To whom have you explained the thread? What happened as a result?
- Have you ever let go of the thread? If so, what happened? And when, if at all, did you regain hold of it?
- Who in your life has encouraged you to hold on to your thread in the midst of challenges and despair? How did they assist you?

Part Three

Practicing the Sacred Art of Conversation

PRACTICING THE SACRED ART OF CONVERSATION

Cultivating Attention, Receptivity, and Compassion Through Conversation

The soul empties itself of all its own contents in order to receive into itself the being it is looking at, just as he is, in all his truth.

—*Simone Weil,* Waiting for God

Ten days before his death, in a televised interview, twentieth-century spiritual teacher, activist, and author Rabbi Abraham Joshua Heschel was asked if he had a special message for young people. He replied: "Remember, that there is meaning beyond absurdity. Know that every deed counts, that every word is power.... Above all, remember that you must build your life as if it were a work of art."[1] Foundational to the work of art that Heschel lived was his relentless commitment to practicing awe, reverence, and gratitude for all of God's creation. In his spiritual anthology, *I Asked for Wonder*, he describes the many ways in which his own life was blessed with the gift of wonder.

Approaching our conversations as a spiritual practice and one another's lives as works of art is the primary aim of this book. In her thought-provoking essay, "Practice Makes Reception," art professor Joanna Ziegler reminds us:

> To approach art with a desire to grasp it fully is to approach it with reverence for what is divine in human creation and with the conviction that it has the power to lift us above the mundane and make us aware of the mystery and wonder of the human spirit. To do so is demanding: it requires discipline, practice, and preparedness.[2]

In an effort to cultivate and instill concentrated awareness in her students' daily routines, Ziegler required them to visit a local museum and to write one paper a week on the same painting for the entire semester. She discovered, "Through repeated, habitual, and direct experience ... students were transformed from superficial spectators, dependent on written texts for their knowledge, into skilled, disciplined beholders with a genuine claim to a deep and intimate knowledge of a single work of art—and they knew it. Moreover, they learned that with practice, any work of art could be accessible to them on its own terms."[3] Through this weekly practice, a tangible transformation unfolded in her students' way of seeing—from narcissistic, willful interpretations to beholding truths about a painting on its own terms.

What if we gave ourselves an assignment similar to the one Joanna Ziegler gave her students? Instead of visiting a museum each week to look upon the same piece of art, what if we initiated a conversation with the same person each week for ten or more weeks? This assignment might prove especially intriguing if we were to try it out with someone we believe we know well, someone who just like a painting we perceive to be static and unchanging. It might be our spouse, a coworker, a neighbor, a parent, or one of our children. Is it possible that we too could move from our self-centered, willful interpretations to beholding truths about others on their own terms?

In this section we'll explore three practices for cultivating greater presence in our conversations with others: attentive presence, receptive presence, and compassionate presence. To apply these practices requires discipline and a commitment to keep practicing. My hope is that you'll begin to see that your continual practice prepares and equips you to behold and see more of those with whom you share conversations on their own, rather than your own, terms.

CHAPTER SEVEN

PRACTICING ATTENTIVE PRESENCE

LISTENING WITHIN BEFORE SPEAKING OUT

Wherever you go, go with all your heart.

—*Confucius*

Wherever we go, if our intent is to practice conversation as a sacred art, we go with all our heart. Our conversations with others provide us an opportunity to listen from the depth of our hearts, to speak the truth of our hearts, and to bring the peaceful presence that flows from our heart's center into our encounter. In this chapter we'll explore the practice of attentive presence. Cultivating attentive presence invites us to attune ourselves to the spirit in the depth of our hearts and in others, to speak from this place of presence and to invite others to do the same, and to try to balance our inner and outer awareness as we engage in conversation.

ATTUNING OURSELVES TO SPIRIT

> *We can either be empty with Spirit or full of ourselves.*
>
> —*Kabir Helminski,* Living Presence

> *There is a voice within you which no-one, not even you, has ever heard. Give yourself the opportunity of silence and begin to develop your listening in order to hear, deep within yourself, the music of your own spirit.*
>
> —*John O'Donohue,* Anam Cara

I remember a time in my life, during my late teens and early twenties, when I evaded facing my inner, silent self. In truth, I just couldn't function without the TV or radio or some kind of background noise. These noises helped distract me from the anguish of the loneliness I was feeling. The thought of slowing down and getting quiet sounded like a form of torture to me, like being placed in solitary confinement. What I wish I had known then is that unless we take the risk of facing our inner silent self, we may never become acquainted with the songs our heart yearns to sing. However, through the sacred art of conversation, we can encourage one another to listen within and become acquainted with the music of our own spirit.

Thomas Merton, the twentieth-century monk and prolific writer, observes:

> Our culture is one which is geared in many ways to help us evade any need to face this inner, silent self. We live in a state of constant semi-attention to the sound of voices, music, traffic, or the generalized noise of what goes on around us all the time. This keeps us immersed in a flood

> of racket and words, a diffuse medium in which our consciousness is half diluted: we are not quite 'thinking,' not entirely responding, but we are more or less there. We are not fully *present* and not entirely absent; not fully withdrawn, yet not completely available.[1]

THE PAUSE THAT CONNECTS

On the first and third Fridays of each month, I meet over the noon hour with a small group of two women and three men. We have no formal agenda to cover, and we begin our meeting with silence.

We have discovered that a few minutes of shared silence at the beginning of our time together helps us shift our attention from the busyness of our mornings to the here and now of the moment. Moreover, our time in shared silence invites us to pause and attune ourselves to our hearts and to one another. After this shared pause, whoever is serving as facilitator for the day reads a poem she or he has selected. We reflect on the poem in silence, and we then take turns sharing what the poem evokes for us.

Our conversation is not a discussion; there is no cross-talk back and forth among us. Rather, each of us has typically five to ten minutes of uninterrupted time to share the truth of our hearts. As one of us speaks, the rest of us do our best to practice attentive presence, that is, as we listen to each other, we listen within. After a person is finished sharing, we pause together once again in silence before responding to him or her. Pausing in silence increases the likelihood that our responses will come from the core of our being, our hearts, rather than from the top of our heads. Sometimes we say very little in response to what another has shared. Our attentive presence says it all. Other times we offer questions with the intent of encouraging the speaker to listen more deeply for the truth being revealed in his or her heart.

Our pacing and process is deliberate. Each of us has a turn to speak, to be listened to, to receive a response from other group members, and to name what we are noticing within us. This rhythm of silence, sharing, silence, responding, continues over the course of the ninety minutes we share together. We then close as we began—in shared silence. Intermingled in all of this quiet and repose is a whole lot of laughter, joy, and, at times, tears. Our time together is teaching each of us a more contemplative way of participating in a conversation. We are learning that there are times when conveying our presence to one another doesn't depend upon words. In fact, we often find that we experience a deeper sense of connection in our times of shared silence.

In our conversations with others, pacing is everything. A nonstop, rapid exchange of words requires that we focus all of our attention outside of ourselves in order to keep up. In such cases, rather than listening to what others are saying, we may find ourselves impatiently waiting for our turn to talk. We talk at, and perhaps talk past, others rather than talk with one another. It's as if one person lights a match in an effort to ignite a conversation and the others blow it out with all their hot air. Rather than creating the synergy of a shared flame, we all end up holding our extinguished matchsticks.

A large part of the sacred art of conversation is learning to practice the pause that connects. Intentionally allowing time to pause and breathe deeply before a conversation begins increases our capacity to pause and listen within throughout a conversation. Devoting time to pause and reflect at the conclusion of a conversation invites all participants to notice and name which aspects of the conversation were particularly significant for them. Practicing the pause that connects does indeed offer the potential to connect us on all levels—to the sacred music of our own spirit, to the sacred in one another, and to the sacred between us.

SPEAKING HEART TO HEART

It is better to be silent and real than to talk and be unreal.
—Saint Ignatius of Antioch

Do not speak unless you can improve upon the silence.
—Quaker saying

In each and every conversation, whether it's unscheduled and ad hoc or a dialogue we've planned for weeks, we have a choice: we can conceal the truth of our hearts or we can reveal ourselves to others and speak from our hearts. Imagine a spectrum where at one end you are speaking from the shallows of your ego or your false self—about what you have, what you do, and what others think of you. At the other end, you are consistently speaking from the depth of your heart and trying to reveal your true self—what your dreams are, what you value, what gives your life purpose and meaning.

In every encounter, whether we're aware of it or not, we navigate this tension between our limited self—our ego—and the fullness of our being—our soul. Our ego is concerned with impressing others and comparing ourselves with them. If you're in a conversation with people who are ego-based, you'll find quickly that they are more interested in what they have to say than what you have to say. If they do ask any questions, you feel as if you're being pumped for information as they judge, assess, and compare themselves to you. Such conversations can drain us, leaving us longing for the conversation to end. Conversely, our soul is concerned with expressing its deepest truth and encouraging others to do the same. If you're in a conversation with people who are speaking soulfully from the heart, you'll find that they are as interested in you, if not more, than they are in themselves; that their questions draw you out; that you feel a sense of unconditional positive regard; that you find yourself energized; and that you lose track of time. We need to keep paying attention to which conversation partners improve our reception to the music of our spirit as well as those who interfere with it.

Although we can't control another person's approach to conversation, nor fully understand his or her intent or motivation, our aim is to cultivate awareness of our own behavior in a conversation. In discerning what to say, how much to say, and how to say it, Sufi imam Jamal Rahman advises: "Make it a habit in everything you say or do to ask yourself, 'Does my speech or action derive from a place of divine attribute within me: truth, love, compassion, beauty? Or do they spring from a place of the little self in me: fear, pettiness, jealousy?'"[2]

BALANCING OUTER AND INNER AWARENESS

The sacred art of conversation invites us to cultivate our consciousness of the conversation occurring on two levels—both the exterior conversation with one or more persons and the interior conversation in the core of our being. To do so, we are invited to pause, breathe deeply, and connect with our heart center. Then we set our intention to listen with the ear of our heart, to speak the truth of our heart, and to bring a nonjudgmental peaceful presence from our heart into our encounter. The divine dwells deep and the more we consciously "drop to our heart" before and throughout a conversation, the more presence we will bring to the conversation. With practice, we may find that trying to maintain awareness of our heart center while focusing on others feels less like an intermittent shift and more like a simultaneous stance of awareness. Our heart center becomes less about a place we go to or a place we come from and more our way of being. We become a listening heart.

Practice: Three Deep Breaths

In his book, *Three Deep Breaths*, aikido master and author Thomas Crum describes the importance of taking three deep breaths, and their related intentions, before beginning an activity:[3]

- The Centering Breath: Breathe in the present moment with balance and energy.
- The Possibility Breath: Breathe in the "me I want to be" with power and purpose.
- The Discovery Breath: Breathe in the Mystery, let go of judgment.

To practice conversation as a sacred art, we too must cultivate the habit of taking three deep breaths, either alone or with others, before a conversation in order to:

- Focus our inner awareness on our heart center and our outer awareness on those with whom we will be speaking;
- Set our intention for the conversation, attune ourselves to the voice within us and within others, and speak from this place of presence and invite others to do the same; and
- Affirm our commitment to maintain a stance of wonder, rather than judgment, as we listen within and to others.

The practice of taking three deep breaths, along with the following practice of centering on our breath, helps cultivate awareness of our heart's subtle frequency. Attuning ourselves to the depth of our heart before a conversation increases the likelihood that we will respond from our heart in the midst of the conversation. It also increases our capacity to speak from our heart and to notice our heart's internal signals in the midst of a conversation.

Practice: Centering on the Breath

The following practice can be done alone or with others. When practicing with others, it is helpful to have someone ring a chime to signal the beginning and ending. A minimum of five minutes is recommended.

> Begin breathing slowly and deeply. Close your eyes, and notice your breathing. Adjust the position of your body so that you are seated in an alert and receptive posture. Since slouching impedes the flow of the breath entering and exiting the body, sit in a way that enables your lungs and diaphragm to fully receive and to fully release the breath. Notice as the breath enters into your nostrils, moves through your throat into your chest, and descends into your abdomen. Notice too how without any effort on your part, the breath then moves outward. Without any effort on your part, your breathing both refreshes your body and releases tension. Continue to notice the gift of this capacity to breathe in and breathe out.
>
> As you breathe, place your hands on your heart. Notice the vibration and energy emanating from your heart. Notice the energy that moves both *in* your heart and *through* your heart.
>
> Continue to breathe at your own pace. As your mind wanders, and it will, gently return to your breath.
>
> Once you have made the connection between breathing and centering, you will find countless ways to practice it. Throughout your conversation and throughout your day, keep returning to awareness of your breathing for refreshment and renewal.

CHAPTER EIGHT

PRACTICING RECEPTIVE PRESENCE

WELCOMING ALL THAT WE ENCOUNTER

A good host is the one who believes that his guest is carrying a promise he wants to reveal to anyone who shows genuine interest.

—*Henri Nouwen,* Reaching Out

It was an auspicious day. It was my first day of graduate school and I had finally secured a spot in one of George Shapiro's classes. This beloved professor did not say a word as he entered the classroom. Rather, he set his worn-out briefcase on the desk and took out a book, announced the title of a passage—hospitality between teachers and students—and began reading. Something about what he read moved me deeply, and I went out after class and bought the book. Since then I have read and reread Henri Nouwen's *Reaching Out: The*

Three Movements of the Spiritual Life. I've also included it as required reading for a number of courses that I have taught. From Nouwen I have learned that to be a good host is to "offer a space where people are encouraged to disarm themselves, to lay aside their occupations and preoccupations and to listen with attention and care to the voices speaking in their own center."[1] Nouwen also helped me name my mission as an educator and a conversation partner: to be a good host.

Some years later I was blessed to have the opportunity to teach at a Benedictine college. It was during my time there that I learned much more about the Benedictine value of hospitality and its emphasis on the practice of welcoming guests. Saint Benedict (480–547 CE) in his rule describes a particular vision of the monastic journey lived in community. I remember being struck by the following phrase from Benedict's rule when I read it for the first time: "All guests who present themselves are to be welcomed as Christ" (RB 53:1).

In reading Benedict's admonition I wondered: who is my guest? So often we refer to a visitor, a temporary occupant, as a guest. Yet, clearly the practice of hospitality was not intended for visitors only. It's often far easier to extend hospitality to visitors, especially when we are assured they are temporary occupants. At least for me, the true test of practicing hospitality is with those I encounter in my daily life. There are times when I find it easier to see the face of Jesus in a stranger than in the faces of those with whom I live and work. Nonetheless, I do find it a perennial challenge to welcome the stranger, the other, as if I were welcoming Jesus. I empathize with the lawyer who asked Jesus, "And who is my neighbor?" and was told that he, like the Samaritan, must show mercy to one and all (Luke 10:25–37). No exceptions.

How would our behaviors toward others change if we assumed that all persons we meet are guests who carry a promise they want to reveal? In this chapter we'll explore three qualities of a good host and how we might cultivate a receptive presence in our conversations with others. Good hosts offer a space where people are encouraged to disarm themselves and share their stories. Good hosts practice welcoming all that they encounter in a conversation—other persons and emotional disturbances. When conversations get difficult, good hosts turn to wonder, and confront their guests in a manner that encourages mutual exploration rather than judgment.

OFFERING A SPACE WHERE PEOPLE ARE ENCOURAGED TO DISARM THEMSELVES

> *In any situation in life, confronted by an outer threat or opportunity, you can notice yourself responding inwardly in one of two ways. Either you will brace, harden, and resist, or you will soften, open, and yield. If you go with the former gesture, you will be catapulted immediately into your smaller self, with its animal instincts and survival responses. If you stay with the latter regardless of the outer conditions, you will remain in alignment with your innermost being, and through it, divine being can reach you. Spiritual practice at its no-frills simplest is a moment-by-moment learning not to do anything in a state of internal brace.*
>
> —*Cynthia Bourgeault,*
> The Wisdom Way of Knowing

If our aim is to be a good host and to create a space where others feel encouraged to disarm themselves, perhaps the best place for us to begin is by paying attention to how we respond to specific persons and topics in our everyday conversations.

With whom or about what topics do we notice ourselves bracing, hardening, and resisting? With whom or about what topics do we notice ourselves opening, softening, and yielding?

The temptation to "armor up" is strong for most of us raised in our individualistic Western world. We tend to take care of me and mine—ourselves and our immediate network of belonging—observe Laurent Parks Daloz, Cheryl Keen, James Keen, and Sharon Daloz Parks. These authors studied people committed to the common good in an effort to understand better the factors that led them to transcend the boundary of "me and mine" and develop connections with the other—those outside of their immediate network of belonging. In their book, *Common Fire: Leading Lives of Commitment in a Complex World*, they report that "a constructive, enlarging engagement with the other"[2] kindles this common fire. Although many of us have daily opportunities for engagement with the Other (e.g., someone of a different nationality, ethnicity, or faith tradition), we need to cross a threshold for an  encounter to be constructive. Although it typically takes more than one meeting, the more that we get to know "others"—their stories and lived experience—the more we recognize that they have fears, joys, yearnings, sufferings, hopes, and loves just as we have. As we forge this recognition of shared experience of feeling, our boundaries expand. We grow in the conviction that everyone counts. We grow to recognize that "seeing resemblance in difference does not mean blurring the distinctions that constitute the integrity of the particular, nor denying differences that are difficult or repugnant."[3] The perception of difference does not prevent us from connecting with and being moved by another's pain.

Johannes Baptist Metz, in his brief yet profound book, *Poverty of Spirit*, believes that in order to create a welcoming space for others, we must begin by forgetting ourselves:

"Every genuine human encounter must be inspired by poverty of spirit. We must forget ourselves in order to let the other person approach us. We must be able to open up to the other person, to let that person's distinctive personality unfold—even though it often frightens or repels us. We often keep the other person down, and only see what we want to see; then we never really encounter the mysterious secret of their being, only ourselves."[4] Metz reminds us that a hospitable conversation is never all about me and mine. Paradoxically, in order to forget ourselves and welcome others, we must begin by cultivating hospitality for ourselves.

CULTIVATING HOSPITALITY FOR SELF: WELCOMING ALL OUR GUESTS

Our capacity to practice a receptive presence stems from our willingness to welcome all of our guests. In the following poem, thirteenth-century Sufi poet and mystic Jalāl al-Dīn Rumi compares our human condition to a guest house.[5]

The Guest House

This being human is a guest house.
Every morning a new arrival.

A joy, a depression, a meanness,
some momentary awareness comes
as an unexpected visitor.

Welcome and entertain them all!
Even if they're a crowd of sorrows,
who violently sweep your house
empty of its furniture,
still, treat each guest honorably.
He may be clearing you out
for some new delight.

The dark thought, the shame, the malice,
meet them at the door laughing,
and invite them in.

Be grateful for whoever comes,
because each has been sent
as a guide from beyond.

For Rumi, our guests are not limited to human visitors. He implores us to "treat each guest honorably." He encourages us to increase our attentiveness to all the *guests* that pay us a visit—our likes and dislikes, hopes and joys, fears and yearnings, and our suffering. In particular, Rumi's poem challenges us to become mindful of the guests who appear uninvited, especially those persons or emotions that we find difficult to receive.

In *Together We Are One: Honoring Our Diversity, Celebrating Our Connection*, Buddhist monk Thich Nhat Hanh identifies two aspects of mindfulness practice. The first aspect is to cultivate our attention to all the wonderful and beautiful things around us, in others, and within us in order to nourish them. The second aspect of mindfulness practice is to get in touch with the difficult emotions around us and within us—our feelings of anger, fear, pain, and sorrow. He encourages us to cultivate mindfulness of our own and others' suffering in order to heal and transform it.

As we learn how to open our minds and our hearts, to soften and yield in the midst of suffering rather than bracing and resisting it, our hospitality for self and others grows. We cannot avoid suffering in this world, but we can incorporate that suffering into our minds and hearts more readily if we can embrace one of the fourteen precepts of Buddhism that suggests we "not avoid contact with suffering or close our eyes before suffering. Do not lose awareness of the existence of suffering in the life of the world. Find ways to be with those who are suffering, including personal contact, images, and sounds. By such means, awaken yourself and others to the reality of suffering in the world."[6]

Confronting Our Guests: Moving from Certainty to Curiosity

> *When we want to be really hospitable we not only have to receive strangers but also to confront them by an unambiguous presence, not hiding ourselves behind neutrality but showing our ideas, opinions and life style clearly and distinctly.... We can enter into communication with the other only when our own life choices, attitudes, and viewpoints offer the boundaries that challenge strangers to become aware of their own position and to explore it critically.*
>
> —*Henri Nouwen,* Reaching Out

"We need to talk." I'm unable to hear or say those four words without my stomach tightening and my blood pressure increasing. As hosts, our primary aim is to receive all our guests and help them reveal the promises they bring. As Nouwen also reminds us, there are inevitably times in almost every relationship where a good host needs to confront a guest. When others see things differently than we see them, don't understand or care about our feelings, or do not realize what a situation means to us, we need to talk to and confront our guests.

Of course, in our culture confrontation has a negative connotation. That's why I appreciate the following definition by Evelyn and James Whitehead: "The ability to confront involves the psychological strength to give (and to receive) emotionally significant information in ways that lead to further exploration

rather than to self-defense."[7] How might we let others know that our intention when we confront them is to invite them to mutually explore a difficulty rather than to attack or blame them for it?

In their book, *Difficult Conversations: How to Discuss What Matters Most*, Douglas Stone, Bruce Patton, and Sheila Heen of the Harvard Negotiation Project underscore the importance of inviting those with whom we disagree to shift to a learning stance. Like the Whiteheads, they recommend that in opening any conversation in which we confront another we invite the other into a joint exploration. In order to do that, they remind us that each difficult conversation is really three conversations:[8]

1. The *"What Happened?" Conversation* that typically involves disagreement about what has happened or what should happen.
2. The *Feelings Conversation,* which may not be addressed directly but leak in anyway.
3. The *Identity Conversation* that we each have internally about what this situation means to us.

It's challenging to remain receptive, to not brace, and to embrace another in the midst of difficulty. Stone, Patton, and Heen recommend that we try to move from a stance of certainty about our side of the story to a stance of curiosity about another's side of the story. To practice a stance of curiosity, in order to better understand another's perspective related to each of the three realms of conversation, we might ask:

- Regarding "what happened or what should happen": "How do you see things?"
- Regarding feelings: "How are you feeling about all of this?"

- Regarding identity: "Say more about why this is important to you."

"Help me to understand." Good hosts begin their conversations with these four words in an effort to learn more about the other. In the midst of difficulty, they turn to wonder rather than judgment. Whenever there are different perspectives in a conversation, a good host seeks to understand better how others see things, their feelings, and why their position is important to them.

Reflection: The Three Gates[9]

The Sufis capture this idea, of how to respond in a difficult situation, in a splendid metaphor. They advise us to *speak only after our words have managed to issue through three gates.*

- At the first gate we ask ourselves, "*Are these words true?*" If so, let them pass on; if not, back they go.
- At the second gate, we ask, "*Are they necessary?*" Our words may be true, but it doesn't follow that they have to be uttered; our words must serve some meaningful purpose. Do our words clarify the situation or help someone? Or, do our words strike a discordant or irrelevant note?
- At the last gate we ask, "*Are they kind?*" If we still feel we must speak out, we need to choose words that will be supportive and loving, not words that embarrass or wound another person. If not chosen with great care, words can have a destructive impact on the consciousness of the person who uses them.

Practice: The Welcoming Prayer

One of the most helpful practices for cultivating mindfulness of our feelings and allowing them into our open consciousness is the welcoming prayer. The welcoming prayer not only cultivates mindfulness of what causes us suffering, but it also clarifies our intention about suffering. Our intention is not to will-*fully* overcome and eliminate all our disturbing thoughts and feelings once and for all. It's also not a will-*less*-ness to dissociate from that which distresses us through prayer. Rather, the welcoming prayer cultivates *our willingness to be vulnerable* and encounter ourselves in order to increase our familiarity with all that visits us in our guest house.[10]

Reverend Cynthia Bourgeault writes about the Christian practice of the welcoming prayer in her book, *Centering Prayer and Inner Awakening*. In a chapter devoted to this practice, she encourages us to practice this prayer as soon as we become aware of an emotional disturbance. The practice consists of three steps: focusing, welcoming, and letting go.[11]

- Begin by *focusing on what is disturbing you and let it sink in*. Become physically aware of the energy as sensation in your body. Try to locate the feeling of disturbance in your body. Although this is often challenging at first, we typically grow in our awareness of how certain emotional states have patterned locations in our bodies. The purpose of such focusing is to remember to stay with whatever is painful rather than trying to change anything. Bourgeault reminds us that the intent of the prayer is not to analyze why we feel the way we do; instead, we want to experience the unpleasant feelings and integrate them.
- *Welcome the feeling of disturbance* as you would a visitor who brings an important message for you. In one or two words, name your experience, for example,

"Welcome anxiety" (or whatever the emotion is), or if it's physical pain, for example, "Welcome aching shoulder." Bourgeault observes:

> *Admittedly, this teaching is paradoxical. Common sense tells you that the unruly emotion is the problem and the solution is to eliminate it. But by welcoming it instead, you create an atmosphere of inner hospitality. By embracing the thing you once defended yourself against or ran from, you are actually disarming it, removing its power to hurt you or chase you back into your smaller self.*[12]

Stay with the feeling to see if some deeper understanding of it emerges or if welcoming it shifts the intensity or quality of the feeling. This is often easier said than done. However, the more you experiment with this type of prayer the more you may find yourself less gripped by a disturbance, and more able to just focus on what is happening within you. A clarifying note: When we welcome the disturbance as if it were a guest, *we are welcoming the physical or psychological content in this moment, not the situation.* For example, if someone is yelling at you, you're not condoning verbal abuse. Rather, what you are welcoming is the feeling of fear or anger or vulnerability that arises in you. You are seeking alignment with the Spirit of God within, not committing to passivity in the midst of confrontation.

- The closing step, if it seems possible, is to *let go* of whatever the named feeling is: "I let go of my anxiety, just for now, not forever" or "I give my anxiety to God." Letting go doesn't suggest that you will not take action in the outer world or passively accept unjust, intolerable situations. Rather, by cultivating awareness of your feeling states, you are increasing your conscious capacity to choose how to respond rather than limiting yourself to unconsciously and compulsively reacting in a given situation.

The welcoming prayer practice is a method for cultivating an inner attitude of receptivity. The welcoming prayer invites us to stay in place rather than fight, freeze, or flee when someone says something that disturbs us. Like an aikido practitioner, we find that rather than strengthening the force of an emotion by pushing it away, if we align with a disturbing feeling and name it we are less likely to be overcome by it. Moreover, this prayer offers us a way of working with the array of disturbances we encounter in our everyday life. The more we practice welcoming what disturbs us, the less likely we are to project our unwelcome thoughts and emotional disturbances on to others. With time and practice, we begin to notice that our capacity to soften, open, and yield slowly begins to grow.

CHAPTER NINE

PRACTICING COMPASSIONATE PRESENCE

GOING WITHIN BEFORE VENTURING OUT

Perhaps the most important thing we ever give each other is our attention. And especially if it's given from the heart. When people are talking, there's no need to do anything but receive them. Just take them in. Listen to what they're saying. Care about it. Most times caring about it is even more important than understanding it.... One of my patients told me that when she tried to tell her story people often interrupted to tell her that they once had something just like that happen to them. Subtly her pain became a story about themselves. Eventually she stopped talking to most people. It was just too lonely.

—*Rachel Naomi Remen,* Kitchen Table Wisdom

The transition to adolescence is a trying time for most of us. My own was accentuated by finding myself in an entirely different terrain. I felt like a refugee in a strange land. No longer was I the little girl in a midwestern Catholic school who sat at the front of the class and loved to read at Mass; I was now one of hundreds in a public junior high school in the suburbs of Phoenix. My peers made fun of the way I talked: "Minne-soh-tan." I missed my home, school, and extended family in Minnesota, and especially my dad who now lived in California. When anyone asked how I liked living in Arizona, I promptly replied: "When I'm eighteen, I'm moving back to Minnesota and going to college at the University of Minnesota." I wanted to make sure that everyone knew where my true home was. Nonetheless, like all adolescents, I yearned for belonging. My teachers were the ones who consistently helped me see new possibilities for belonging.

I remember the day when my home economics teacher, Ms. Mosher, invited me to stay for lunch in her classroom. Although I don't remember anything she said, because she intentionally didn't say much, I vividly recall her presence. She never looked at her watch and didn't seem concerned about what she had to do next. Rather, she was all there with me in the moment. I don't know whether Ms. Mosher made it a habit to seek out students who seemed unhappy, and I don't recall that we ever talked at length again. Yet, what has stuck with me after all those years was her willingness to share her attention so lavishly. She wasn't being paid to do so. I have since met with other professional helpers, from counselors to spiritual directors, and few have matched the gift of attentiveness I received that day. That is why I try to keep my antennae up for those Ms. Mosher encounters with my own students. When you receive a gift like that, you are eager to pass it on.

Ms. Mosher is one of many people in my life who have embodied compassionate presence. She seemed to know that when people are talking there's no need to do anything but receive them. Just take them in. Listen to what they're saying. Care about it. Most times caring about it is even more important than understanding it. In this chapter we'll explore the practice of compassionate presence in the sacred art of conversation. In particular, we'll look at two expressions of compassion in conversations: compassionate commiseration (holding our own and others' pain) and compassionate responding (inviting others to listen within).

COMPASSIONATE COMMISERATION: HOLDING OUR OWN AND OTHERS' PAIN AND DIFFICULTY

Our hurting friends need our silence, not our speeches.
—*Robert Kellemen and Karole Edwards,*
Beyond Suffering: Embracing the Legacy of African Americans

"Life is difficult." With these three words, psychiatrist M. Scott Peck begins his book *The Road Less Traveled*. He observes:

> "Once we truly know that life is difficult—once we truly understand and accept it—then life is no longer difficult.... Most do not fully see this truth that life is difficult. Instead, they moan more or less incessantly, noisily or subtly, about the enormity of their problems, their burdens, and their difficulties as if life were generally easy, as if life *should* be easy."[1]

We, too, hear the moaning, the problems, the burdens, and the difficulties of others in the conversations we share with them. As we listen, we tend to feel a very real pressure to alleviate others' struggles, solve their problems, and help them get on with their lives. In an effort to empathize, we may even share our own experience of a similar difficulty. Nonetheless, we often feel ill-equipped and never know quite what to say. We are in a dilemma—unsure how to respond to another's pain when we don't quite know what to do with our own.

> *If only we arrange our life according to that principle which counsels us that we must always hold to the difficult, then that which now still seems to us the most alien will become what we most trust and find most faithful.... Why do you want to shut out of your life any agitation, any pain, any melancholy, since you really do not know what these states are working upon you?*
>
> —*Rainer Maria Rilke,* Letters to a Young Poet

How might our conversations be different if we arranged our way of responding in accordance with Rilke's principle of holding to the difficult? What if we paid attention to our struggle instead of venting it or repressing it and invited those we encounter to do the same?

Some twenty-five hundred years ago, the Buddha articulated his first noble truth: life is suffering. Buddha believed that suffering can be noble if we learn how to look deeply into the nature of suffering rather than run away from it. Indeed, suffering not only cultivates understanding; it can cultivate compassion for self and others. Jesus also expressed this profound truth. He taught that it is only through suffering, through dying to self, that we can experience the fullness of life: "Very truly, I tell you, unless a grain of wheat falls into the earth and dies, it remains just a single grain; but if it dies, it bears much fruit"

(John 12:24). The fruits of selfless love can emerge from suffering. Sufi master Hazrat Inayat Khan affirms this truth: "God breaks the heart again and again and again until it stays open."[2]

The difficulties and suffering we experience in our lives can indeed break us open, yet they can also shatter us and shut us down. The experience of suffering in our lives depends in large part upon whether or not we have others who are willing to accompany us through the inevitable heartbreaks we experience. We all need wise conversation partners who know, as a result of their own suffering, that becoming intimate with pain can be transformative. Wise conversation partners encourage us to practice "staying open to everything we experience, letting the sharpness of difficult times pierce us to the heart, letting these times open us, humble us, and make us wiser and more brave."[3] Wise conversation partners have the capacity to help us hold on in the midst of difficulty, because they have practiced holding their own pain and difficulty. Wise conversation partners also encourage us to listen within to the Eternal Listener.

GO WITHIN BEFORE VENTURING OUT

> *Do not run, but be quiet and silent. Listen attentively to your own struggle. The answer to your question is hidden in your own heart.*
>
> —*Henri Nouwen,* Reaching Out

One of the finest contemporary examples of someone who practiced listening attentively both to his own struggle and to the struggles of others is Howard Thurman (1899–1981). Thurman, one of the great preachers of the twentieth century, served as a spiritual advisor to many in the civil rights movement, including Martin Luther King Jr. He advised to "go within" before "venturing out." Listening to one's own struggle is challenging for most of us, and especially so for victims of oppression (many of whom have deliberately concealed their feelings in order to survive). Yet, Thurman knew from his own experience of deep listening in contemplative prayer that going within helped him face and move against injustice. He believed that by rooting ourselves in and living from God, we develop our inner authority.[4] In his beloved book, *Meditations of the Heart*, he writes:

> There is in every person an inward sea, and in that sea there is an island and on the island there is an altar and standing guard before that altar is the "angel with the flaming sword." Nothing can get by that angel to be placed upon that altar unless it has the mark of your inner authority. Nothing passes "the angel with the flaming sword" to be placed upon your altar unless it be a part of "the fluid area of your consent." This is your crucial link with the Eternal.[5]

> *One of the tasks of true friendship is to listen compassionately and creatively to the hidden silences. Often secrets are not revealed in words, they lie concealed in the silence between the words or in the depth of what is unsayable between two people.*
>
> —*John O'Donohue,* Anam Cara

This past spring I attended a silent retreat. Each day consisted of periods of sitting and walking meditation, a presentation in the morning and evening, chanting, and quiet unscheduled time. Aside from the opening meal, conversation among participants was not allowed.

On Good Friday, the day that commemorates the crucifixion of Jesus, we were encouraged to devote the hours between noon and three to silent prayer in the oratory. Christians believe that it was during this particular time of day that Jesus suffered and died on the cross. As I entered the oratory after lunch that day, I found only one other person there. I took a seat on "my" cushion and began to settle into my breathing. Shortly thereafter, I heard the door to the oratory open and close. I was aware that others had joined us. Not much time had passed before I heard someone sobbing, really sobbing. It's not unusual to shed tears on Good Friday. However, I did notice that the sobbing persisted and didn't seem to abate. I peeked out of the corner of my right eye to assess the situation. It was clear that something was moving deeply in this sister retreatant, and yet she seemed all right. Nonetheless, I find it very difficult to listen to and stay with another's anguish. No matter who it is or where I am, my mind returns to the times I saw or heard my mother crying. And when it does, I still experience the sense of helplessness I felt as a child and a very real need to try to do something to alleviate another's pain. However, the training I received in spiritual direction taught me to not follow my inclination *to do something*, such as reach out and touch another's hand or offer words of comfort. Instead, we were encouraged to remain present and prayerfully hold a space for the other to move deeper into his or her experience. And so that is what I tried to do that afternoon in the oratory. I tried to remain present and hold the space for the sobbing retreatant. To symbolize this, I moved my hands from the center of my lap to my knees and turned my palms upward.

On Easter Sunday morning, the day that commemorates the resurrection of Jesus, we broke our silence and celebrated this great Christian feast. Although the twenty of us had connected at a very deep level through our time in shared silence, we were eager to talk with one another. One of the first persons to approach me that morning was Mary, the woman who had been sobbing in the oratory on Good Friday. Mary came up and told me that she wanted to thank me. She then described how much it had meant to her to have me in the oratory with her that afternoon. She said she could sense my presence and could sense that my concern for her was palpable. She let me know that both the tears and the experience of feeling held by me and others was one of the most precious gifts she received from the retreat. I in turn thanked her. I told her that although I had wanted to reach out and comfort her, I didn't want to interfere with or impede her from paying attention to what was being revealed in her heart.

It was challenging just to sit there and listen to another person sobbing, presumably in pain. I felt confused and uncertain as to how to best respond. Yet, my intent was to respond in a compassionate manner rather than merely react in a way that would alleviate my own anxiety. So, what I tried to do that afternoon was to practice compassionate abiding so that I could stay in place and discern the most appropriate course of action.

Compassionate abiding, like sacred holding, is a practice that encourages us to "go within before venturing out." If we are able to *go within* and abide with what we find difficult or dislike, we are less likely to react impulsively when we *venture out* and more likely to respond compassionately. Guidelines for both of these practices can be found at the end of the chapter.

COMPASSIONATE RESPONDING: INVITING OTHERS TO LISTEN WITHIN

> *No other person can ever chart a course for you, but a friend and a host who is really present can at times firm up what you in your own deepest heart of hearts have already felt drawing at you.*
>
> —*Douglas Steere,*
> On Being Present Where You Are

One of my most memorable experiences of compassionate listening occurred during a retreat I facilitated with a group of college students. We were practicing together an alternative way of responding to one another—compassionate responding. Rather than problem-solving and advice-giving, we were trying to listen one another's souls into disclosure and discovery. We were inviting each other to firm up what we felt drawing at us in our deepest heart of hearts.

I told the group about a prayer experience I had had a number of years ago that I was still struggling to make meaning of. When the prayer experience occurred, I had just made a major professional transition. I had resigned from a teaching position and begun consulting work in the nonprofit sector. In an effort to discern better what God was calling me to next, I attended a one-week silent retreat. Throughout the course of the week, I was disappointed that no specific guidance had yet emerged. During my time in prayer on the last evening of the retreat, I noticed how my mind kept imagining how I might create different types of educational projects. It was in the midst of that imagining that I heard the words "partners in production." Since I don't typically hear specific words during my prayer time, these three words really captured my attention.

After I finished telling my story of this prayer experience, the students had some time to work together in triads in order to generate a compassionate response. I was amazed at their ability to acquire this skill so readily. Rather than telling me what they thought these words might mean for me or suggesting that I consider persons in my life with whom I might strike up a partnership, one trio asked me the following question: "What meaning do the words you heard then hold for you today?" Their question invited me to listen deeply within and consider what these words had meant to me then, over the course of the ensuing years, and what they meant for me now. Although their question didn't resolve my ambiguity and uncertainty, it invited me to pay attention to my hopes and dreams and yearnings in the here and now.

In her book, *Listening Spirituality*, Quaker teacher Patricia Loring observes that:

> There may be no more tellingly difficult spiritual practice than the effort to receive what is being said by someone else hospitably, without editing, without correction, without unsolicited advice. Yet, it is this open listening that makes room for the Spirit of God to be present in the midst of the interaction, illuminating and guiding what is taking place. With grace, the Holy Presence is born into the space that we make by giving over our own agendas: God with us, a third presence in our encounter.[6]

Loring reminds us that as we listen ...

- We don't need to demonstrate that we are intelligent, clever, or profound;
- We aren't responsible for straightening out people whose viewpoints differ from our own or whom we perceive to have deficient information;

- We don't need to prove that we are actively listening by offering encouraging remarks or relaying similar or pertinent experience;
- We aren't responsible for healing people who are in pain or difficulties by any means other than simply being present for them.[7]

The more that we grow in awareness of our habitual way of responding, and practice simply being present for others, we find:

> As the listener really listens not only to the content, but for the movement of the Spirit under the content, the speaker also may be drawn into awareness of deeper levels of her utterance. Held long enough in this receptive, listening prayer, the speaker may begin to give over the need to create a particular impression, to entertain, to be interesting, to evoke a particular response. She may begin to go below the usual socially structured level of discourse to speak more profound truths, usually hidden or obscured by conformity to expectations of others.[8]

In her book, *The Sacred Art of Listening*, Kay Lindahl suggests that as we discern how to respond to one another, we shift our focus from "'What do I want to say?' (from the ego) to 'What wants to be said?' (from the soul)."[9] In any conversation, there are times we need to step up and contribute more and times we need to step back and practice restraint. In most conversations I usually have at least one observation or piece of advice that I want to share. And, I have to really sort out my motivation before doing so: Is it that I want to demonstrate what I know in the hopes that others will think I'm an intelligent and caring person? Or is it that I am experiencing a nudge in my heart that something wants to be said? If I'm struggling to discern whether or not to say something, I usually wait. If what I had intended to say keeps coming back to me, and seems to be coming from the core of my being, I offer it. However, if what I had intended to say doesn't persist or no longer seems to fit with the flow of conversation, I just let it go. If our aim is to respond soulfully and compassionately, rather than superficially and compulsively, we benefit from not speaking words on the tip of our tounge or thoughts off the top of our head until we've taken time to let such sentiments descend to our heart. Before we respond, we are invited to "center down," that is, to shift our consciousness from our head to the cave of our heart where the Divine Center dwells. From there, as we learn to listen with the ear of our heart, we grow to recognize the difference between *what we want to say* and *what wants to be said through us*. In some cases, *what wants to be said through us* may not need to take the form of words. Our listening presence is more than enough.

Practice: Offering the Gift of Contemplative Questions

Compassionate responding offers us an alternative way of being present to others in conversation rather than our conventional practices of advising, analyzing, or problem solving. Compassionate responding challenges us to go beyond active listening in order to listen contemplatively with our ears, our eyes, our bodies, and the ear of our hearts. Often, the most compassionate response we can offer others is to listen to them attentively without comment, interruption, or interjection. Our aim is to remain present, listening to the sacred stirrings within our heart as we simultaneously listen to another. As we do, we may notice a question gently arising. Instead of asking the first question that comes to mind, we discern: What can I ask this person, in such a way, that will invite him or her to listen more deeply within?

One of the finest resources for learning how to create the conditions for listening another's soul into disclosure and discovery is Parker Palmer's *A Hidden Wholeness*. In this book he offers invaluable guidance for framing questions to offer others. True to his Quaker formation, Palmer stresses that we allow ourselves time to pause in order to begin to absorb what we have heard before responding and that whatever we ask be gently paced, brief, and to the point. He also recommends that our questions be open and honest, that they:[10]

- expand rather than restrict a person's arena of exploration. For example, if a person is struggling to find a job, you might ask: "Of the jobs you've applied for, what aspects of them do you find yourself most interested in?" rather than "How many resumes have you sent out this month?"
- do not presume a "right answer." For example, if a person is struggling with marital difficulties, you might ask: "When you both are at your best, how do you feel about your marriage?" rather than "Have you met with a marriage counselor to discuss this?"
- are guided by the language a speaker uses. For example, if a person is describing the challenges he is experiencing in discerning his life's purpose, you might ask: "What are you feeling jazzed about in your life these days?" rather than "What is God calling you to do?"
- are motivated by caring, not one's own curiosity. For example, if a person is describing her difficulties praying, you might ask: "What activities increase your awareness of the sacred?" rather than "What prayer methods have you tried?"

Practice: Sacred Holding

Transformation can potentially occur if we are willing to go within and be present to our feelings of fear, disappointment, anger, and grief. The Sufis refer to this stance as trembling and believe that trembling has the potential to shake open our heart and connect it to Heart. Imam Jamal Rahman describes in his book, *The Fragrance of Faith*, what he learned from his grandfather about the importance of tending a trembling heart. He reminds us that not all experiences of trembling are beneficial; "only when you take the trembling steps with compassion for yourself, does the trembling become sacred." Rahman refers to this practice of tending a trembling heart as sacred holding.

Sacred holding is a method for cultivating compassion for oneself. Like the Christian welcoming prayer we considered in the previous chapter, this practice invites us to notice, name, and nurture awareness of all our feelings, especially the negative ones, rather than impulsively express, repress, or obsess about them.

- Begin by allowing yourself to experience the feeling of disturbance and then to name it.
- After naming the feeling, try to locate where you are holding the feeling in your body. Encompass the physical sensations in your body with the embrace of your soul. From your heart, send love and mercy to this place in your body.
- Talk tenderly to yourself; cultivate a gentle rapport with yourself. Rahman suggests that you might want to tell yourself: "I'm sorry you feel this.... This is difficult.... Let me tenderly support you...." Rather than trying to fix or analyze the sensations or the feelings, simply be present for as long as you want. This is the process of trembling. Focus gently on the holding in your body,

inhale and exhale through that part of you. Allow divine breath to caress you there.[11]

Compassionately tending our trembling hearts through sacred holding is a spiritual practice that invites us to pay attention to what disturbs us rather than to try to fix it. We are encouraged to cultivate compassion for ourselves rather than judge ourselves or analyze why we feel the way we do. Aside from the comfort and healing this practice can offer us personally, attending to and tending our own trembling hearts shows us a way of attending to and tending others.

The practice of sacredly holding our own pain prepares us to practice holding a space of compassion for others. As Buddhist monk Thich Nhat Hanh reminds us:

> *It doesn't matter if we've had their experience. What matters is that we can listen, and that we can listen well enough that their experience can be healed and transformed. So a lot of it is about the power of simply listening and holding a space of compassion for people sharing their difficulties, their pain, their insights. A lot of that can be done without saying a word, just by staying in touch with your own breathing and making sure your own heart stays open.*[12]

Practice: Compassionate Abiding

Like sacred holding, compassionate abiding is another approach for bringing warmth to unwanted feelings. In her book, *Taking the Leap: Freeing Ourselves from Old Habits and Fears*, Buddhist nun Pema Chodron introduces us to this Buddhist practice. She encourages us to put this into practice as soon as we notice we're disturbed by something or someone.

- Begin by getting in contact with the disturbing experience by breathing in and opening to the feeling. Breathe in such a way that helps you abide with the feeling instead of pushing it away. The invitation is to contact the feeling without interpreting it.
- Then, "as you breathe out, relax and give the feeling space. The out-breath is not a way of sending the discomfort away but of ventilating it, of loosening the tension around it, of becoming aware of the space in which the discomfort is occurring."[13]

The focus on breathing in this practice emphasizes the importance of ventilating our feelings in an effort to transmute their energy. Imagine being in a room filled with windows. On a hot day, we need to open the windows and ventilate the room with fresh air. If we don't, we get more heated up and experience greater anguish. Similarly, in the midst of experiencing heated, difficult emotions, we need to open the windows and ventilate our inner room with fresh air through our breathing. Chodron explains that by breathing in and opening to disturbing feelings rather than acting them out, we reduce the seeds of aggression within us.

CONCLUSION

Do not call to mind the former things, or ponder
things of the past
Behold, I will do something new,
Now it will spring forth;
Will you not be aware of it?
—*Isaiah 43:18–19A,* New American Standard

Like a good conversation, I'm finding it difficult to bring this book to a close. I've noticed, as I listen to the conversation in my heart, more themes I would like to explore—for example, how our conversations invite us to bless and be blessed, to seek to understand and be understood, to scatter and receive joy. I've also noticed the increasing number of articles and books about communication. Many focus on the challenges of communicating in our digital age as we continue to discern the best ways to make use of the growing number of devices and platforms for connecting with one another. Others document discoveries being made by neuroscientists and the increasing evidence to support the distinctive benefits of face-to-face communication. In particular, I take comfort in reading about the value of *internal* education, which "promotes the active exploration of first-person subjective experience." The core curriculum for internal education consists of a new set of R's: resilience, reflection, and relationships.[1] I relish learning about terms such as "time-in" and how imperative it is to our brain's development that we devote time "to focus inward, to pay attention to our sensations, images, feelings, and thoughts as we *SIFT* the mind's inner experience. Taking time-in each day can promote improvements in emotion regulation, attention, and empathy."[2] I smile as I imagine future generations of parents and teachers encouraging children to take a "time-in." Clearly, there is far more that I could explore related to this sacred art of conversation. Yet, I recognize that it is time to bring this book to a close. And so I'll conclude, as I began, with a story.

More than thirty years ago, I returned from Phoenix to my beloved home state of Minnesota. Since then, whenever I travel to Phoenix to visit my mother and extended family, I have established a tradition of making a pilgrimage to my favorite independent bookstore, Changing Hands. Each visit to this particular bookstore becomes a pilgrimage because, without exception, upon each visit there a book finds me. As I walk my customary path through the various sections of the store, carefully perusing the shelves, *it* appears—a title that I wasn't previously aware of and one that I didn't set out to find.

Recently, Mark and I traveled to Phoenix to celebrate my mother's seventy-fifth birthday. During that visit, not unlike previous ones, I left Changing Hands with an armful of books. However, I only brought *the* book with me on the airplane. While en route back to Minneapolis, it was with great anticipation that I began perusing Diane Eshin Rizzetto's book, *Waking Up to What You Do.* I read a chapter or two and then turned to chapter six which opened with this epigraph taken from T.S. Eliot's *The Cocktail Party*. "At every meeting we are meeting a stranger."[3] The words seemed to jump off the page. I set the book down and paused to take some deep breaths. I then picked the book up and began reading the chapter titled:

"I take up the way of speaking of others with openness and possibility". As I read, I thought to myself, this precept would have been great to include in my book. However, I had just sent the final manuscript to my editor. I finished the chapter, passed the book to Mark and said, "Read this." (Mark and I thrive on discussing books. It all started on our first date with *Zen and the Art of Motorcycle Maintenance*.) So, being the great husband that he is, he set down his iPad, took the book from my hands, and read the chapter. As he handed the book back to me, I asked, "Isn't that amazing? Imagine if we could consistently put that into practice: to meet others as strangers." He nodded.

> *When we meet others as strangers, our hearts are open to possibility, change, and reconciliation. We haven't decided what one another is, and only know that person as she presents herself in this very moment. Yesterday, you may have exchanged a few harsh words and thought her disagreeable but today, in this moment, where is disagreeable? I like to think of our faultfinding as tinted glasses obscuring a clear view of who or what we meet at any given time. If you meet that person with the words of yesterday echoing in your mind, then your glasses are tinted disagreeable. You cannot meet the other as the stranger. How do we assume or not assume that a person has changed since yesterday? As long as we insist on seeing him through our memories, those glasses will not allow us to meet him openly and with possibility.*
>
> —*Diane Eshin Rizzetto,*
> Waking Up to What You Do

Meeting the stranger invites us to continually press the refresh button on our perceptions of others and ourselves. Rizzetto underscores the paradoxical nature of meeting the stranger. "In order to truly know someone, we have to be open to the possibility of change, and admit that we can only truly know that person in the present moment."[4] Although it's never easy, I often find it less difficult to meet a literal stranger *openly and with possibility* than to meet the stranger in those with whom I live and work. Moreover, it's only in the past couple of years that I've grown to appreciate the strangeness I encounter in myself, those parts of me that are new and unfamiliar. I know I'm not alone.

We tend to freeze our perceptions of others and ourselves rather than encounter the unknown and unfamiliar. "You know how men *are*, they're clueless about feelings." "Oh, that's just how Aunt Sherice *is*; the only person she's concerned about is herself." "I *am* too emotional. I'm afraid I'll never get a job in sales because I can't take rejection." We can blame it on our brains. Neuroscientists are discovering that the natural tendency of our brains is to take an idea or action that is unfamiliar to us and reconceive it as something we are already familiar with. For example, if I have never met a man who has disclosed his feelings, I may reject the notion that men want to and therefore never consider inviting any man to do so. If I perceive Aunt Sherice to be self-absorbed because she has never inquired about my life or offered to do anything for me, I may overlook or fail to notice behaviors that counter my view. If I believe that I am so emotional that anyone's rejection will cause me to crumble, it isn't likely that I'll recall times when I haven't.

Throughout this book, I've invited us to cultivate our awareness of what is being revealed in our heart, in another's heart, and in between us as we engage in conversation. As I reflect upon what I have written, I increasingly realize that the sacred art of conversation is a spirituality of beholding and meeting the stranger. As the opening epigraph from the Hebrew Scriptures reminds us, the Spirit is beckoning us to behold, to be aware of, the *something new* in ourselves, in others, in our relationships, and in our world. We are practicing the sacred art of conversation whenever we encourage one another to behold, to be on the lookout for the myriad ways in which the sacred is springing forth in our lives—both those that seem familiar and especially those that appear to be strange.

And so, even though I had thought this book was finished, I noticed how this theme of meeting the stranger kept recurring in the conversation in my heart and in conversations with my husband. Over the past month since we've been back home, at various points throughout our daily conversations, Mark grins and then interjects:

> "It's about the stranger, right?"
>
> I respond with delight, "Yep, it's about the stranger."

This book is now finished, but the conversation continues....

Appendices

The Sacred Art of Conversation in Community

CREATING OCCASIONS FOR CONTEMPLATIVE CONVERSATIONS

I definitely feel there are many listening ears in our society and many people eager to use their voices in ways that lead to questions and wonder. I feel that hunger every place I go, and I feel a receptivity in our culture to that hunger.

—*Naomi Shihab Nye*

The thirteenth-century poet and Sufi mystic Jalāl al-Dīn Rumi speaks of two kinds of intelligence. We acquire the first kind of intelligence, consisting of facts and concepts, from outside of ourselves—most often from books and teachers. However, we can only acquire the second type of intelligence from within. It's a "tablet, one already completed and preserved inside you. A spring overflowing its springbox. A freshness in the center of the chest."[1] The Sufis believe that the best way to awaken this second type of intelligence—the Divine Essence in each person—is to gather in a circle with a small group of others.

In these appendices we'll explore approaches for gathering in small groups to awaken this inner intelligence as we practice the sacred art of conversation. What distinguishes these contemplative conversations from other forms of conventional small group gatherings is the emphasis they place on silence. It is more than coincidence that the words *silent* and *listen* share the same letters. There is a profound relationship between intentional silence and our capacity to listen. It is only by getting quiet, really quiet, that we notice all the noise within, between, and around us as we interact with one another. Time in silence, both personal and collective, helps us to discern the sacred signals from all the other sounds in our lives. Silence is a foundational practice for any meaningful conversation and one that is particularly fitting for interfaith dialogue. Silence is a spiritual practice that transcends and can unite participants of varying faith traditions, cultures, and ways of life.

Parker Palmer, who specializes in creating the conditions for small group conversations he calls "circles of trust," underscores the transformative power of silence:

> The soul is like a wild animal—tough, resilient, savvy, self-sufficient, and yet exceedingly shy. If we want to see a wild animal, the last thing we should do is go crashing through the woods, shouting for the creature to come out. But if we are willing to walk quietly into the woods and sit silently for an hour or two at the base of a tree, the creature we are waiting for may well emerge, and out of the corner of an eye we will catch a glimpse of the precious wildness we seek.[2]

If we hope to have more soulful conversations with one another, we need to practice walking quietly, sitting silently, and waiting patiently.

APPENDIX ONE

CULTIVATING CONTEMPLATION AND COMPASSION IN COMMUNITY THROUGH JOURNEY CONVERSATIONS

Reach out to those you fear.
Touch the heart of complexity.
Imagine beyond what is seen.
Risk vulnerability one step at a time.
—*Jean Paul Lederach,* The Moral Imagination

What is a journey conversation? A journey conversation creates an occasion to explore life's big questions in the company of others: What is sacred in my life? What's my purpose? What difference can I make? In a journey conversation participants are invited to slow down, turn off their electronic devices, and learn ways of listening within and listening to one another. Participants embark on a journey of mutual discovery as they share their stories and encourage one another to notice and name what they hold sacred in the midst of the struggles, contradictions, and ambiguities of their lives. Sharing fundamental life stories helps participants see both the commonality in the midst of their diversity and the distinctive features of their common experiences. Participants also engage in a journey of discernment as they learn how to ask contemplative questions that help each other notice and name where they find meaning and purpose in their lives. In some communities, a journey conversation may also include time devoted to collective discernment as groups and teams reflect upon what gives their organization meaning and purpose. What is distinctive about this approach to dialogue is the emphasis it places on contemplative practices as the foundation for relational communication: practices of silence, stillness, and centering; sacred reading; storytelling; compassionate listening and responding.

This appendix will provide an overview of the processes and structures developed for hosting and facilitating journey conversations and describe the fruits of these conversations.

JOURNEY CONVERSATION FORMAT OVERVIEW

In a journey conversation participants are invited to turn from their conventional way of interacting and are introduced to contemplative practices and communication skills that help them listen deeply, speak from their heart, and respond compassionately. *Stillness and centering practices* encourage participants to listen within; *the practice of storytelling* invites them to listen to their lives; and *the practice of compassionate listening and responding* increases their capacity to listen and learn from one another.

The format and process of hosting a journey conversation is highly adaptable. The following format has been tested in a wide array of contexts with men and women of varying ages, faiths, and ethnic backgrounds.

Centering Practices

Contemplative practices, such as shared silence, stillness, and centering on the breath, prepare participants for conversation. Some groups find it helpful to place a glass container filled with water in the center of the circle. This transparent container of water symbolizes the group's purpose and commitment. Like the still water that reflects what it encounters, the group's aim is to create a contemplative container where participants can practice being so still that others can see the reflection of their deepest truths in one another's presence. Some groups also place a candle at the center of the circle to symbolize the light of the divine within and among those gathered.

The primary role of the facilitator is to cultivate this contemplative awareness and rhythm. Facilitators begin each gathering by inviting participants to take some time to quiet their minds and bodies, to remove any unnecessary distractions around them, and to turn their attention to their breathing. They lead the group through the practice of three deep breaths (see page 75) or centering on the breath (see page 76). Throughout the conversation, facilitators try to be mindful of the group's need to periodically pause in silence in order to maintain or regain attentive presence.

In addition, facilitators are responsible for minding the time so that every person has time to speak. They encourage those who find it difficult to speak to listen within for a spiritual nudge to speak; encourage those who feel compelled to speak to practice restraint if there are gaps in the conversation; and gently remind one and all to honor the transformative power of shared silence.

Sacred Reading

Once participants have quieted themselves through centering practices, they are invited to listen deeply to wisdom literature including scriptures from the world's religious traditions, contemporary prose and poetry. Listening to wisdom that is born from the lived experience of ancient and modern people and communities prepares the group to notice and welcome the wisdom that lives in each member of the group.

The facilitator introduces the contemplative practice of *lectio divina*. This approach to reading scripture was practiced by Benedict of Nursia (480–547 CE) who served as a founder of Western monasticism. The practice of *lectio divina* invites participants to *listen with the ear of their heart* as they encounter the transformative power of the written word.[3]

- The first time the text is read, the facilitator invites participants to listen for a word, a phrase, or an image that shimmers for them or captures their attention.
- After the first reading, each participant is invited to offer his or her word or phrase into the silence without comment.
- The second time the text is read, the facilitator invites participants to reflect upon what is being asked of them or offered to them by the text.
- After the second reading, participants are invited to briefly share their responses with the rest of the group.

STORYTELLING

When a group first forms, each participant is invited to reflect upon, construct, and share the story of his or her journey: the key events, persons, places, and experiences; their understanding of the sacred and how that has changed over the course of their lives; and their deepest hopes for their relationship with what they deem to be sacred in their lives. If a group continues to meet on a regular basis, participants may select or design additional themes for their storytelling (such as the conversation catalysts in appendix three). Perhaps the most significant aspect of reflecting on one's story is the realization that our stories are always open to new interpretation. Each time we listen to our lives, we have the opportunity to discover, notice, and name more fully what we hold to be sacred. To help participants begin to construct a narrative of their journey, they are asked to reflect upon the following questions:

> If my life were a book, I would title it
>
> ______________________________.
>
> The reasons I give my life this title are
>
> ______________________________.
>
> The chapters in the book of my life are
>
> ______________________________.
>
> The chapter I am in right now is
>
> ______________________________.
>
> As I imagine the next chapter on my journey,
> I would name it ____________________.

To model the storytelling process, we ask group facilitators to share their stories first. As they do, we encourage them to describe to participants their process for reflecting upon and constructing their narrative.

Compassionate Listening and Responding

The primary aim in compassionate listening and responding, as the Quaker Douglas Steere emphasized, is to "listen each other's soul into disclosure and discovery."[4] Following each person's story, participants are invited to offer the gift of contemplative questions. Instead of asking the first question that comes to mind, each participant is encouraged to discern carefully: What can I ask this person that will invite him or her to listen more deeply within?

The following diagram compares a conventional way of asking questions with a more contemplative stance:

Conventional Questions	Contemplative Questions
What do I want to say? (ego)	What wants to be said? (soul)
Often seek to fix, save, analyze, or advise another	Seek to understand and learn more about another
Closed-ended questions (can you, have you, would you, is there, etc.) that can be answered "yes," "no," or in a few words.	Open-ended questions that begin with: how, what, where, when or "in what ways ..."
Elicit reactions	Evoke reflection
May or may not resonate with another's experience	Resonate with another's experience
Often guided by the language you use	Are guided by the language another uses
Restrict another's arena of exploration	Expand another's arena of exploration
Allow for the exchange of information	Encourage another to keep noticing, naming, and nurturing his or her awareness of God/sacred

Facilitators remind participants that asking contemplative questions is often a new and countercultural skill. A journey conversation group offers the opportunity to practice and cultivate this skill, as we learn with and from one another. In some cases, we discern it is best to not ask another person a question, as our attentive silent presence is what seems to be most needed.

COLLECTIVE REFLECTION

Conversations conclude with some time for quiet to reflect upon what has been shared. Participants are then invited to notice and name what they have discovered in the course of the conversation.

Participants may find it helpful to reflect upon and respond to one or more of the following questions:

- What did you notice in today's conversation?
- What stirred you or moved you deeply?
- What did you learn about yourself or others in today's conversation?

Some groups may also choose to conclude the conversation with a closing prayer. Whether or not a prayer is used, all group gatherings conclude with time in shared silence. The facilitator may ring a chime to signal the close of the session. However, some participants may prefer to continue to sit in silence while others take leave.

JOURNEY CONVERSATION PARTICIPANT AGREEMENTS

The first session of every new group begins with an overview of the participant agreements. These provide the ground rules for the conversation. The facilitator's role is to model the following skills and attitudes and hold participants accountable to them.

As a participant:

- I will listen to others in a compassionate and non-judgmental way. I will also strive to *listen within*, noting my internal responses to what is being said.
- I will speak for myself, in the first person, as I relay my experiences, feelings, perceptions, attitudes, and beliefs (for example, "I feel ...," "I sensed that ...,"

"I wonder about ..."). I will speak the truth of my heart as I offer the insights, joys, struggles, and questions that are part of my journey.

- I will encourage and honor my own and others' questions. I recognize that it is not my responsibility to analyze, fix, save, or advise others in the group.
- I will observe time limits. I will arrive on time. I will limit my storytelling and sharing to the time allotted.
- I will feel free to remain silent and tell the group if I would like to pass.
- I will maintain "double confidentiality." What is shared in the group stays in the group. Moreover, I will not approach any of our group's participants with feedback or advice outside of our meeting times unless it is asked for.
- I will speak directly to a group participant if a conflict arises or if clarification about something s/he said is needed.

Facilitators ask participants if they have any questions about the agreements and invite them to name agreements they would like to add. Other agreements?

- ____
- ____
- ____

Some communities may invite participants to sign the agreement. Many facilitators return to the agreements at subsequent sessions in an effort to remind participants of the covenant they have made with one another.

Facilitators then invite participants to identify their hopes for the conversation (whether it's a one time meeting or an ongoing series). Through our conversations, we hope to:

- ____
- ____
- ____

Many groups have found it beneficial to return to their listed hopes periodically, to reflect upon their process, and to refine or refresh their stated hopes.

Starting a Journey Conversation in Your Community: Frequently Asked Questions

What is the optimal size for a journey conversation group?

Five to seven participants in a small group seems to work best in most settings. However, in some settings, we have facilitated large groups of forty or more participants. In those situations, we gather the entire group for the centering practice and sacred reading, break into small groups of four to five participants for storytelling and contemplative questions, and reconvene in the larger circle for the concluding reflection.

How often do you meet and what is the optimal amount of time to meet?

The format for a typical contemplative conversation group consisting of ninety minutes is featured below. A ninety-minute gathering allows enough time for two participants to share the stories of their journeys. However, in some retreat and workplace settings, groups may meet only once for a half or full day of conversation. Regardless of the number of participants or duration of the meeting time, the following time frames are the minimum we have found beneficial for each portion of a journey conversation gathering:

> Centering Practice and Sacred Reading
> (15–20 minutes)

Storytelling One (10–15 minutes)

Pause for Silent Reflection (2–3 minutes)

Compassionate Listening and Responding (10–15 minutes)

Pause for Silent Reflection (2–3 minutes)

Storytelling Two (10–15 minutes)

Pause for Silent Reflection (2–3 minutes)

Compassionate Listening and Responding (10–15 minutes)

Pause for Silent Reflection (2–3 minutes)

Collective Reflection (10 minutes)

WHERE DO I FIND TEXTS FOR THE SACRED READING?

Each community or small group selects texts that they find evocative and meaningful. In many groups, participants take turns selecting a text to share with the group. In others, the primary facilitator selects texts aligned with a group's hopes and interests. For example, interfaith groups often choose to reflect upon one sacred scripture from a different religious tradition at each gathering.

FRUITS OF JOURNEY CONVERSATIONS

Journey conversations create the conditions for a different kind of conversation by inviting participants to develop a deeper, interior awareness through contemplative practice in the company of others. Over the course of the past decade, a large part of my work has been devoted to facilitating and training facilitators for journey conversations. My work has also focused on evaluating the impact these conversations are having on participants.

Participants tell us that they place a great value on the contemplative practice of silence and a scheduled time and place to reflect; they no longer believe that a mature faith requires having everything figured out; they have learned a new way of being present to others; and they have experienced a different way of being together in relationship—a spiritual fellowship—through these groups. The following statements illustrate these themes:

- How important it is to slow down and take time for silence? In the past, I often knew this in the back of my head but never did it. Now, I want to incorporate these rhythms into my life to help me center myself.
- I used to think that I was the only one who didn't have it all figured out or who had questions, but I have discovered that I have many of the same doubts and thoughts as others. I have also become more confident with speaking about faith and religion and in the interfaith groups was comfortable discussing such touchy subjects with strangers.
- I'm trying to bring my spiritual thoughts and approaches to discussing spirituality to more of my interactions. Even if conversations and/or actions are not directly aimed at a "spiritual" topic, the skills, care, compassionate questions, and calmness can still be used in many interactions.
- Being able to articulate out loud to others some of my current thoughts, struggles, beliefs, questions, etc. This has helped me personally identify more about my own journey. Also, hearing and reflecting upon others' stories has allowed me to make connections with my group members in a way I normally wouldn't be able to and identify some of the similarities and differences in our journeys.

Although many group participants report feeling initially uncomfortable with, or resistant to, slowing down, getting quiet, and listening within, they describe that it really helps cultivate contemplative listening in the company of others.

It is clear that these conversations are having both a personal impact on participants and a community-building impact on the group. Moreover, many participants report that what they have learned and experienced in a journey conversation is bearing fruit outside of the group setting. Through these conversations, they are cultivating a peaceful listening presence that they try to bring into their everyday activities and relationships with friends, coworkers, and family members.

Gathering with others for a journey conversation cultivates habits, develops skills, and gives us a safe place to practice the sacred art of conversation. Together we are learning another way of talking about faith, meaning, and purpose in our lives. Deeply listening to another's accounts of faith and doubt, belief and skepticism, love and fear often inspires us to give voice to our own. As we reflect upon our journeys together, we often gain new insights and a deeper appreciation of what each person brings to the conversation. Taking the time to gather in silence, to notice and name our experience of the sacred in our lives increases the likelihood that we will enhance our capacity to notice and name even more. Listening to others share their experiences of the sacred nurtures our collective awareness of the sacredness of life, increases empathy and awareness of "others," and builds compassionate communities.

APPENDIX TWO

APPRECIATIVELY FOCUSED CONVERSATIONS AT HOME AND WORK

The glory of God is human being fully alive."

—*Saint Irenaeus*

One of the primary ways we engage one another in the sacred art of conversation is by inviting each other to pay attention to what enlivens us. Our primary aim is to invite one another to notice and name what we experience as life-giving rather than trying to eradicate that which drains us of life. In this Appendix we will consider a specific conversational approach—appreciative inquiry—used by practitioners in the field of organizational development and explore how we might draw upon this approach to enrich our everyday conversations.

In an appreciative inquiry conversation (commonly referred to as AI), participants are invited to focus on life-giving forces. Rather than starting with the problems people are having and trying to fix what's broken, AI practitioners believe that improvement stems from starting with what's working and building upon it. Sue Annis Hammond identifies AI's guiding assumptions in *The Thin Book of Appreciative Inquiry*:[5]

1. In every society, organization, or group, something works.
2. What we focus on becomes our reality.
3. The act of asking questions of an organization or a group influences the group in some way.

The engine that drives the appreciative inquiry process is storytelling. The fuel for the engine is questions.

In conversations with individuals, groups, or a team of organizational stakeholders, those who employ an AI approach pose rich evocative questions that invite respondents to describe in detail specific experiences and the facets of such experiences that they find most enlivening. Rather than frame their questions in a conventional manner that tends to elicit rote rehearsed responses (e.g., how long have you worked here, what do you do, or what do you think of this organization) appreciatively worded questions more often evoke rich responses that help participants notice and name signs of life and energy that they may have forgotten or overlooked.

Appreciatively worded questions are often concerned with three themes: historical—that is, inquiring about a time when things were at their best or an individual had a peak experience; inner-directed—that is, inquiring about an individual's core strengths or values; and future-oriented—that is, inquiring about participants' hopes or wishes for what they'd like to see more of in the future.[6] The following examples illustrate how we might incorporate these questions into our family, workplace, and community conversations.

- A historically focused question:
  - Reflect on your experience as a member of this family, workplace, or community. Recall a time when you felt most alive, spiritually touched, or most excited about your involvement. Tell us about this memorable experience and how it deepened your commitment to your family, workplace, or community.
- Inner-directed questions:
  - What distinctive contribution do you believe you offer to this family, workplace, or community?
  - What is the single most important thing that you'd like to contribute to this family, workplace, or community?
- A future-oriented question:
  - What are three hopes you have for this family, workplace, or community?

After we have invited one another to respond to one or more of these questions, we can then begin to explore how we might cocreate this imagined future together.

APPENDIX THREE

CONVERSATION CATALYSTS

When we reach our innermost heart we reach a realm where we are not only intimately at home with ourselves, but intimately united with others, all others.
—Brother David Steindl-Rast,
Gratefulness, The Heart of Prayer

The following quotations and reflection questions are designed to serve as catalysts for conversations between two or more persons.

Guidelines

- Centering: Begin with some time in shared silence.
- Sacred Reading: Ask a participant to read the quotation one or more times. Pause in silence after the reading has ended.
- Storytelling: Invite one person to begin sharing his or her responses or wait until a person volunteers to do so.
- Compassionate Listening and Responding: After each person responds to the reflection questions, invite him or her to explore the theme further by asking contemplative questions.

- Pause: Take time to honor what has been shared before inviting another person to speak.
- Collective Reflection: After all participants have had a turn responding to the questions, take some time to reflect upon your shared experience:
  - What did you notice in today's conversation?
  - What stirred you or moved you deeply?
  - What did you learn about yourself or others in today's conversation?

Some groups may also choose to conclude the conversation with a closing prayer. Whether or not a prayer is used, allow some time for shared silence. The facilitator will ring a chime to signal the close of the session. However, some participants may prefer to continue to sit in silence while others take leave.

Add to the following set of conversation starters by bringing one or more of your favorite inspirational quotations to share with others in a future conversation.

Always stay in your own movie.

—*Ken Kesey*

- On a scale of one to ten (one being difficult and ten being easy), which number best describes how you feel about "staying in your own movie"? Talk about your reasons for selecting the number you did.
- What title best describes the movie you are currently in?
- If you could snap your fingers and cast yourself in a different movie, what would you name your feature

film? Where would you be living? What would you be doing? With whom would you share your time?

- What does imagining this alternative movie show you about potential next scenes as you "stay in your own movie"?

Joy does not simply happen to us. We have to choose joy and keep choosing it every day.

—Henri Nouwen

- Can you recall a time in your life when joy simply happened to you? If so, tell a story about your experience.
- Have you ever chosen joy? If so, what did you do?
- How, if at all, would your life be different if you chose joy every day?

If the only prayer we could say is thank you that would be enough.

—Meister Eckhart

- Who are the persons in your life for whom you are especially thankful?
- To what extent have you been able to convey your gratitude to them?
- Select one person to whom you haven't yet conveyed your gratitude. What did this person do for you and what have you learned from him or her? How

might you create an occasion to thank the person for what he or she has contributed to your life?

People try to get away from it all—to the country, to the beach, to the mountains. You always wish you could too. Which is idiotic: you can get away from it anytime you like. By going within. Nowhere you can go is more peaceful—more free of interruptions—than your own soul.... Renew yourself. But keep it brief and basic. A quick visit should be enough to ward off all ... and send you back ready to face what awaits you.

—Marcus Aurelius

- When do you most want to escape your life?
- Where do you dream of going?
- Have you ever experienced getting away from it all by going within?
- What helps you or hinders you from going within?

We who lived in concentration camps can remember the men who walked through the huts comforting others, giving away their last piece of bread. They may have been few in number, but they offer sufficient proof that everything can be taken from a man but one thing: the last of the human freedoms—to choose one's attitude in any given set of circumstances, to choose one's own way."

—Viktor Frankl

- Tell a story about a time in your life when you exercised the freedom to choose your attitude in a difficult set of circumstances. Who was involved? What happened? What did you learn from this experience?
- Who in your life has exercised the freedom to choose his or her attitude in a difficult set of circumstances? What have you learned from the person?

The new culture is created by those people who are not afraid to be insecure.

—Rudolph Bahro

- Tell a story about a time in your life when you experienced insecurity.
- What action would you take in your life right now if you could do so with full awareness of your insecurity(ies)?

Our goal should be to live life in radical amazement ... get up in the morning and look at the world in a way that takes nothing for granted. Everything is phenomenal; everything is incredible; never treat life casually. To be spiritual is to be amazed.

—Abraham Joshua Heschel

- What are you finding most incredible and phenomenal in your life at this time?

- What, if anything, do you take for granted?
- What single change could you make in your life to live it with a greater sense of amazement?

Die before you die.

—Muhammad

- Tell a story about a time in your life when you experienced dying to your own needs in order to more fully respond to others' needs. Who was involved? What happened?
- What helps you die to, or let go of, your own concerns, ambitions, and need to be in control?

You must always keep in mind that a path is only a path: If you feel you should not follow it, you must not stay with it under any conditions. To have such clarity you must lead a disciplined life. Only then will you know that any path is only a path, and there is no affront, to oneself or to others, in dropping it if that is what your heart tells you do to. But your decision to keep on the path or leave it must be free of fear or ambition ... look at every path closely and deliberately. Try it as many times as you think necessary.

—Don Juan's advice to Carlos Castaneda

- What is your path at this time in your life?

- What paths have you dropped because your heart told you to do so?
- What helps or will help you look at a path deliberately?

NOTES

Introduction

1. Jon Kabat-Zinn, *Coming to Our Senses: Healing Ourselves and the World Through Mindfulness* (New York: Hyperion, 2005), 147.
2. Sherry Turkle, "The Flight from Conversation," *New York Times*, April 22, 2012, accessed on May 2, 2012, www.nytimes.com/2012/04/22/opinion/sunday/the-flight-from-conversation.html.
3. Margaret Wheatley, *Turning to One Another: Simple Conversations to Restore Hope to the Future*, 2nd ed. (San Francisco: Berrett-Koehler Publishers, 2009), 7.
4. Ibid., 33.
5. Ibid., 29.

Part One
What Is the Sacred Art of Conversation?

1. *On Being*, accessed on June 4, 2012, www.being.publicradio.org/programs/2008/studs_terkel.

Chapter One
Encountering the Sacred Within

1. Susan Scott, *Fierce Conversations: Achieving Success at Work & in Life, One Conversation at a Time* (New York: Viking Penguin, 2002), 83.
2. Used with permission of the poet Jeannie E. Roberts. For more information, visit www.jrcreative.biz.
3. Wayne Teasdale, *The Mystic Heart: Discovering a Universal Spirituality in the World's Religions* (Novato, CA: New World Library, 1999), 53.

CHAPTER TWO
ENCOUNTERING THE SACRED IN EACH OTHER

1. Thomas R. Kelly, *A Testament of Devotion* (New York: HarperSanFrancisco, 1992, originally published New York: Harper & Brothers, 1941).
2. Patricia Loring, *Listening Spirituality: Personal Spiritual Practices Among Friends* (Washington, DC: Openings Press, 1997), 161.

CHAPTER THREE
ENCOUNTERING THE SACRED BETWEEN US

1. Sandy Eisenberg Sasso, *God in Between* (Woodstock, VT: SkyLight Paths, 1998), 21, 25, 29, 32.
2. Rabbi Dennis Ross, in his book *God in Our Relationships*, offers an inspirational introduction to Buber's philosophy of I and Thou. Through an array of stories and practical examples, he shows us how this theology of relationships can be applied in our everyday lives. See Rabbi Dennis Ross, *God in Our Relationships: Spirituality between People from the Teaching of Martin Buber* (Woodstock, VT: Jewish Lights, 2003).
3. "PBS NewsHour," accessed on October 2, 2012, www.pbs.org/newshour/bb/entertainment/july-dec10/herbie_09-16.html.

PART TWO
GATEWAYS FOR CONVERSATION

1. William Stafford, *The Way It Is: New & Selected Poems* (Minneapolis, MN: Graywolf Press, 1998), 42.
2. Janet Ruffing, *To Tell the Sacred Tale: Spiritual Direction and Narrative* (Mahwah, NJ: Paulist Press, 2011), 106–7.

CHAPTER FOUR
LISTENING TO YOUR LIFE

1. John O'Donohue, *To Bless the Space Between Us: A Book of Blessings* (New York: Doubleday, 2008), 49.
2. Margaret Wheatley, "Perseverance," accessed on September 16, 2010, www.margaretwheatley.com/articles/Perseverance-GulfOfMexico.pdf.
3. Parker J. Palmer, *Let Your Life Speak: Listening for the Voice of Vocation* (San Francisco: Jossey-Bass, 2000), 3–4.

4. Frederick Buechner, *Now and Then: A Memoir of Vocation* (New York: HarperOne, 1983), 87.
5. Ibid., 3.
6. See Richard L. Hester and Kelli Walker-Jones, *Know Your Story and Lead with It: The Power of Narrative in Clergy Leadership* (Herndon, VA: Alban Institute, 2009).
7. Jill Freedman and Gene Combs, *Narrative Therapy: The Social Construction of Preferred Realities* (New York: W.W. Norton, 1996).
8. Freedman and Combs, *Narrative Therapy*, 98.
9. Ira Progroff, *At a Journal Workshop: Writing to Access the Power of the Unconscious and Evoke Creative Ability*, rev. ed. (New York: G.P. Putnam's Sons, 1992).
10. Dave Isay, *Listening Is an Act of Love: A Celebration of American Life from the StoryCorps Project* (New York: Penguin, 2007), 1.
11. See Freedman and Combs, *Narrative Therapy*, 42–76, for more information on deconstructive listening and questioning and opening space for new stories.
12. Hester and Walker-Jones, *Know Your Story and Lead with It*, 35.

CHAPTER FIVE
NOTICING AND NAMING WHAT GIVES YOU LIFE

1. "PBS NewsHour," accessed on October 6, 2012, www.pbs.org/newshour/bb/entertainment/july-dec04/kooser_10-21.html.
2. Ted Kooser, *Winter Morning Walks: One Hundred Postcards to Jim Harrison* (Pittsburgh, PA: Carnegie Mellon University Press, 2001).
3. Ted Kooser, *The Poetry Home Repair Manual: Practical Advice for Beginning Poets* (Lincoln, NE: University of Nebraska Press, 2005), 14.
4. Ted Kooser, *Local Wonders: Seasons in the Bohemian Alps* (Lincoln, NE: University of Nebraska Press, 2004).
5. Jim Brandenburg, *Chased by the Light*, 2nd ed. (Minneapolis, MN: Creative Publishing International, 2001).
6. Gregory Wolfe, "Stalking the Spirit." *Image: Art, Faith, Mystery* (2011): 3–6.
7. Evelyn Underhill, *Practical Mysticism* (Alpharetta, GA: First Ariel Press, 1986; originally published in 1914), 109.
8. Ann Patchett, *What Now?* (New York: HarperCollins, 2008), 22.

9. Simone Weil, *Waiting for God* (New York: HarperCollins, 2009; originally published New York: G.P. Putnam's Sons, 1951).
10. Dennis Linn, Sheila Fabricant Linn, and Matthew Linn, *Sleeping with Bread: Holding What Gives You Life* (Mahwah, NJ: Paulist Press, 1995), 7.
11. Ibid., 34.
12. Tad Dunne, *Spiritual Mentoring: Guiding People through Spiritual Exercises to Life Decisions* (San Francisco: HarperCollins, 1991), 90–91.
13. John Fox, *Poetic Medicine: The Healing Art of Poem-Making* (New York: Jeremy P. Tarcher/Penguin, 1997), 228.

CHAPTER SIX
DISCERNING A HEART-CENTERED PATH

1. John O'Donohue, *Beauty: The Invisible Embrace: Rediscovering the True Sources of Compassion, Serenity, and Hope* (New York: HarperCollins, 2004), 147.
2. Margaret Silf, *Inner Compass: An Invitation to Ignatian Spirituality* (Chicago: Loyola Press, 1999), 64.
3. Jack Kornfield, *A Path with Heart: A Guide through the Perils and Promises of Spiritual Life* (New York: Bantam Books, 1993), 12.
4. Jamal Rahman, *The Fragrance of Faith: The Enlightened Heart of Islam* (Bath, England: Book Foundation, 2004), 57.
5. John Neafsey, *A Sacred Voice Is Calling: Personal Vocation and Social Conscience* (Maryknoll, NY: Orbis Books, 2006).

PART THREE
PRACTICING THE SACRED ART OF CONVERSATION

1. Abraham Joshua Heschel, *I Asked for Wonder: A Spiritual Anthology*, ed. Samuel Dresner (New York: Crossroad, 1996), 21–22.
2. Joanna Ziegler, "Practice Makes Reception: The Role of Contemplative Ritual in Approaching Art," in *As Leaven in the World: Catholic Perspectives on Faith, Vocation, and the Intellectual Life*, ed. Thomas M. Landy (Lanham, MD: Sheed & Ward, 2001), 33.
3. Ibid., 39.

CHAPTER SEVEN
PRACTICING ATTENTIVE PRESENCE: LISTENING WITHIN BEFORE SPEAKING OUT

1. Thomas Merton, *Love and Living* (New York: Farrar, Straus, & Giroux, 1979), 40.
2. Jamal Rahman, *The Fragrance of Faith: The Enlightened Heart of Islam* (Bath, England: Book Foundation, 2004), 48.
3. Thomas Crum, *Three Deep Breaths: Finding Power and Purpose in a Stressed-Out World* (San Francisco: Berrett-Koehler Publishers, 2006), 91.

CHAPTER EIGHT
PRACTICING RECEPTIVE PRESENCE: WELCOMING ALL THAT WE ENCOUNTER

1. Henri Nouwen, *Reaching Out: The Three Movements of the Spiritual Life*. (New York: Doubleday, 1976), 76.
2. Laurent Parks Daloz, Cheryl H. Keen, James P. Keen, and Sharon Daloz Parks, *Common Fire: Leading Lives of Commitment in a Complex World* (Boston: Beacon Press, 1996), 63.
3. Ibid., 77.
4. Johannes Baptist Metz, *Poverty of Spirit* (Mahwah, NJ: Paulist Press, 1968), 43–4.
5. Jalāl al-Dīn Rumi, "The Guest House," in *The Essential Rumi: New Expanded Edition*, trans. Coleman Barks, with John Moyne, A.J. Arberry, and Reynold Nicholson (New York: HarperOne, 2004), 109.
6. Chan Khong, *Learning True Love: How I Learned & Practiced Social Change in Vietnam*. (Berkeley, CA: Parallax Press, 1993), 80.
7. Evelyn Eaton Whitehead and James D. Whitehead, *Marrying Well* (New York: Doubleday Image Books, 1983), 309–319.
8. Douglas Stone, Bruce Patton, and Sheila Heen, *Difficult Conversations: How to Discuss What Matters Most* (New York: Penguin Putnam, 1999), 7–8.
9. Eknath Easwaran, *Meditation: A Simple Eight-Point Program for Translating Spiritual Ideas into Daily Life*, 2nd ed. (Tomales, CA: Nilgiri Press, 1991), 159.

10. Gerald May, *The Awakened Heart: Opening Yourself to the Love You Need* (New York: HarperCollins, 1991), 48–9.
11. Cynthia Bourgeault, *Centering Prayer and Inner Awakening* (Lanham, MD: Cowley Publications, 2004), 143–47.
12. Ibid., 144–5.

CHAPTER NINE
PRACTICING COMPASSIONATE PRESENCE: GOING WITHIN BEFORE VENTURING OUT

1. M. Scott Peck, *The Road Less Traveled: A New Psychology of Love, Traditional Values and Spiritual Growth* (New York: Simon & Schuster, Inc., 1978), 15.
2. Source unknown.
3. Pema Chodron, *Practicing Peace in Times of War* (Boston: Shambhala, 2007), 71.
4. Lerita Coleman Brown, "An Ordinary Mystic: Contemplation, Inner Authority, and Spiritual Direction in the Life and Work of Howard Thurman," *Presence: An International Journal of Spiritual Direction* 18, no. 1 (2012): 19.
5. Howard Thurman, *Meditations of the Heart* (Boston: Beacon Press, 1953), 15.
6. Patricia Loring, *Listening Spirituality: Personal Spiritual Practices Among Friends* (Washington, DC: Openings Press, 1997), 161.
7. Ibid., 172–3.
8. Ibid., 164.
9. Kay Lindahl, *Practicing the Sacred Art of Listening: A Guide to Enrich Your Relationships and Kindle Your Spiritual Life: The Listening Center Workbook* (Woodstock, VT: SkyLight Paths, 2003), 32.
10. Parker J. Palmer, *A Hidden Wholeness: The Journey Toward an Undivided Life* (San Francisco: Jossey-Bass, 2004), 132–138.
11. Jamal Rahman, *The Fragrance of Faith: The Enlightened Heart of Islam* (Bath, England: The Book Foundation, 2004), 109–10.
12. Thich Nhat Hanh, *Together We Are One: Honoring Our Diversity, Celebrating Our Connection* (Berkeley, CA: Parallax Press, 2010), 132.

13. Pema Chodron, *Taking the Leap: Freeing Ourselves from Old Habits and Fears* (Boston: Shambhala, 2009), 90.

CONCLUSION

1. Daniel J. Siegel, *Pocket Guide to Interpersonal Neurobiology: An Integrative Handbook of the Mind* (New York: W.W. Norton & Company, 2012), 43.3.
2. Ibid., 25.2.
3. T.S. Eliot, *The Cocktail Party*, I, iii (London: Faber and Faber, 1950), 72–3.
4. Diane Rizzetto, *Waking Up to What You Do: A Zen Practice for Meeting Every Situation with Intelligence and Compassion* (Boston: Shambhala, 2005), 72.

APPENDICES

1. Jalāl al-Dīn Rumi, "Two Kinds of Intelligence" in *The Essential Rumi*, trans. Coleman Barks with John Moyne, A.J. Arberry, and Reynold Nicholson (New York: HarperOne, 2004), 178.
2. Parker J. Palmer, *Let Your Life Speak: Listening for the Voice of Vocation* (San Francisco: Jossey-Bass, 2000), 7–8.
3. Christine Valtners Painter, *Lectio Divinia—The Sacred Art: Transforming Words & Images into Heart-Centered Prayer* (Woodstock, VT: SkyLight Paths, 2011).
4. Douglas Steere, *Gleanings: A Random Harvest* (Nashville, TN: Upper Room, 1986), 83.
5. Sue Annis Hammond, *The Thin Book of Appreciative Inquiry*, 2nd ed. (Bend, OR: Thin Book, 1998), 20–21.
6. Susan Star Paddock, *Appreciative Inquiry in the Catholic Church* (Plano, TX: Thin Book, 2003), 6.

SUGGESTIONS FOR FURTHER READING

Alexander, Scott. "Knowing and Loving Our Neighbors of Other Faiths," in *On Our Way: Christian Practices for Living a Whole Life*, eds. Dorothy C. Bass and Susan R. Briehl. Nashville, TN: Upper Room Books, 2010.

Bastian, Edward W. *InterSpiritual Meditation: A Seven-Step Process Drawn from the World's Spiritual Traditions*. Santa Barbara, CA: Spiritual Paths Publishing, 2010.

Bourgeault, Cynthia. *Centering Prayer and Inner Awakening*. Lanham, MD: Cowley Publications, 2004.

Cannato, Judy. *Field of Compassion: How the New Cosmology Is Transforming Spiritual Life.* Notre Dame, IN: Sorin Books, 2010.

Chodron, Pema. *Practicing Peace in Times of War*. Boston: Shambhala, 2007.

Cooperrider, David, and Diana Whitney. *Appreciative Inquiry: A Positive Revolution in Change*. San Francisco: Berrett-Koehler Publishers, Inc., 2005.

De Mello, Anthony. *Awareness.* New York: Doubleday, 1990.

Dougherty, Rose Mary. *The Lived Experience of Group Spiritual Direction*. Mahwah, NJ: Paulist Press, 2003.

Edwards, Tilden. *Embracing the Call to Spiritual Depth: Gifts for Contemplative Living.* New York: Paulist Press, 2010.

———. *Living in the Presence: Spiritual Exercises to Open Our Lives to the Awareness of God*. New York: HarperCollins Publishers, 1995.

Finley, James. *The Contemplative Heart.* Notre Dame, IN: Sorin Books, 1999.

Freedman, Jill, and Gene Combs. *Narrative Therapy: The Social Construction of Preferred Realities.* New York: W.W. Norton & Company, 1996.

Griffin, Emilie, and Douglas Steere, eds. *Quaker Spirituality: Selected Writings.* New York: HarperSanFrancisco, 1984.

Hammond, Sue Annis. *The Thin Book of Appreciative Inquiry*, 2nd ed. Bend, OR: Thin Book Publishing Company, 1998.

Helminski, Kabir. *The Knowing Heart: A Sufi Path of Transformation.* Boston: Shambhala, 1999.

———. *Living Presence: A Sufi Way to Mindfulness and the Essential Self.* New York: Penguin Putnam, Inc., 1992.

Hester, Richard, and Kelli Walker-Jones. *Know Your Story and Lead with It: The Power of Narrative in Clergy Leadership*. Herndon, VA: The Alban Institute, 2009.

Isay, Dave. *Listening Is an Act of Love: A Celebration of American Life from the StoryCorps Project.* New York: The Penguin Press, 2007.

Johnson, Aostre N., and Marilyn Webb Neagley, eds. *Educating from the Heart: Theoretical and Practical Approaches to Transforming Education*. Lanham, MD: Rowman and Littlefield Publishers, Inc., 2011.

Kabat-Zinn, Jon. *Coming to Our Senses: Healing Ourselves and the World Through Mindfulness.* New York: Hyperion, 2005.

Kline, Ann. "Widening the Lens: The Gift of Group Spiritual Direction." *Presence: An International Journal of Spiritual Direction* 10, no. 2 (2004): 38–42.

Kramer, Gregory. *Insight Dialogue: The Interpersonal Path to Freedom*. Boston: Shambhala, 2007.

Lederach, John Paul. *The Moral Imagination: The Art and Soul of Building Peace.* New York: Oxford University Press, 2005.

Lindahl, Kay. *Practicing the Sacred Art of Listening: A Guide to Enrich Your Relationships and Kindle Your Spiritual Life.* Woodstock, VT: SkyLight Paths, 2003.

Linn, Dennis, Sheila Fabricant Linn, and Matthew Linn. *Sleeping with Bread: Holding What Gives You Life*. Mahwah, NJ: Paulist Press, 1995.

Loring, Patricia. *Listening Spirituality: Personal Spiritual Practices Among Friends*. Washington, DC: Openings Press, 1997.

Millis, Diane. "Cultivating Compassion through Group Spiritual Companioning." *Presence: An International Journal of Spiritual Direction* 18, no. 3 (2012): 6–14.

Newberg, Andrew, and Mark Waldman. *Words Can Change Your Brain: 12 Conversation Strategies to Build Trust, Resolve Conflict, and Increase Intimacy*. New York: Hudson Street Press, 2012.

Newell, John Philip. *Listening for the Heartbeat of God: A Celtic Spirituality*. Mahwah, NJ: Paulist Press, 1997.

Nhat Hanh, Thich. *Joyfully Together: The Art of Building a Harmonious Community*. Berkeley, CA: Parallax Press, 2003.

———. *Together We Are One: Honoring Our Diversity, Celebrating Our Connection*. Berkeley, CA: Parallax Press, 2010.

Nouwen, Henri. *Reaching Out: The Three Movements of the Spiritual Life*. New York: Doubleday, 1976.

———. *The Way of the Heart*. New York: Ballantine Books, 1981.

O'Donohue, John. *Anam Cara: Spiritual Wisdom from the Celtic World*. London: Bantam Books, 1997.

———. *To Bless the Space Between Us: A Book of Blessings*. New York: Doubleday, 2008.

Palmer, Parker J. *A Hidden Wholeness: The Journey Toward an Undivided Life*. San Francisco: Jossey-Bass, 2004.

———. *Let Your Life Speak: Listening for the Voice of Vocation*. San Francisco: Jossey-Bass, 2000.

Prechtel, Daniel. *Where Two or Three Are Gathered: Spiritual Direction for Small Groups*. New York: Morehouse Publishing, 2012.

Rahman, Jamal. *The Fragrance of Faith: The Enlightened Heart of Islam*. Bath, England: The Book Foundation, 2004.

Reuter, Mary. *Running with Expanding Heart: Meeting God in Everyday Life*. Collegeville, MN: Liturgical Press, 2010.

Ringer, Judy. *Unlikely Teachers: Finding the Hidden Gifts in Daily Conflict*. Portsmouth, NH: OnePoint Press, 2006.

Rosenberg, Marshall. *Nonviolent Communication: A Language of Life*. Encinitas, CA: PuddleDancer Press, 2003.

Ross, Dennis. *God in Our Relationships: Spirituality between People from the Teachings of Martin Buber*. Woodstock, VT: Jewish Lights Publishing, 2003.

Ruffing, Janet. *To Tell the Sacred Tale: Spiritual Direction and Narrative*. Mahwah, NJ: Paulist Press, 2011.

Sacks, Jonathan. *The Dignity of Difference: How to Avoid the Clash of Civilizations.* New York: Continuum, 2003.

Scott, Susan. *Fierce Conversations: Achieving Success at Work & in Life, One Conversation at a Time*. New York: Viking Penguin, 2002.

Siegel, Daniel J. *Pocket Guide to Interpersonal Neurobiology: An Integrative Handbook of the Mind.* New York: W.W. Norton & Company, Inc., 2012.

Silf, Margaret. *Wise Choices: A Spiritual Guide to Making Life's Decisions*. New York: BlueBridge, 2007.

Wheatley, Margaret. *Turning to One Another: Simple Conversations to Restore Hope to the Future*, 2nd ed. San Francisco: Berrett-Koehler Publishers, Inc., 2009.

ACKNOWLEDGMENTS

As a child, I can recall hearing the comment: *You ask so many questions, are you writing a book or something*? I am especially blessed to have two parents, Rosemary and Joseph, who took my questions seriously, along with two younger sisters, Debra and Dana, who kept me from taking myself too seriously. In addition to my family, I have been blessed with many wonderful teachers who showed me that teaching is about far more than relaying a subject matter. Their examples continue to inspire me in my vocation as an educator, and encourage me to keep asking, "What return can I make?"

I can't imagine writing a book on conversation without having a number of wise and discerning conversation partners with whom to test out these ideas and practices. I am especially grateful to Ward Bauman, Tawanna Brown, Sandhya Purohit Caton, Dianne DelGiorno, Jennifer Grant Haworth, Paul Hayes, Patrick Henry, Aostre Johnson, Lucy LaGrange, Amy Zalk Larson, Sheila Radford-Hill, Linda Ricketts, Jeannie Roberts, Rosemary Senjem, Kent Simmonds, and Bob Stains, who read one or more of the book's chapters and shared so generously of their time as we engaged in conversation about them.

I am blessed to have the ongoing opportunity to learn more about the practice of attentive, receptive, and compassionate presence from my spiritual director, Lois Lindbloom, and the members of my spirituality group—Mary Cavanaugh, Mary Freitag, Chris McPartland, Jim Diedrich Smith, and Lew

Zeidner. I am grateful for their accompaniment and the joy they bring to my life.

I knew I had found a tender and wise conversation partner in Emily Wichland at SkyLight Paths Publishing from the first phone conversation we shared. My initial impression has been confirmed throughout the editorial process. I have also had the pleasure of working with Henry Lowell Carrigan, my content editor, whose editorial prowess helped make this a far better book than the one I initially submitted. Last, but by no means least, I was blessed to work with editor Kaitlin Johnstone. It was Kaitlin who helped me navigate all the details in the journey from copy editing to completion. I am especially grateful to the three of them for consistently honoring my voice and for the rest of the team at SkyLight Paths who collaborated with me to make my vision for this book possible.

On the day I met my husband, Mark, in 1984, we began a conversation that I never wanted to end. Over the past twenty-eight years, I have continually witnessed his immense capacity for engaging others in conversation. He is my most treasured conversation partner, and I am so grateful for his enduring love and encouragement of my vocation. I dedicate this book to him and to our son, Ryan, who, in his unceasing commitment to keeping his heart open during the trying times of adolescence, kept reminding me of the fundamental importance of our heart in conversation. Their love and way of being embodies for me the essence of this sacred art.

ABOUT THE JOURNEY CONVERSATIONS PROJECT

Our mission is to introduce more persons to contemplative practices for dialogue; to increase their capacity to notice and name what they hold sacred in their lives; and to prepare and equip more persons to facilitate contemplative conversations.

We work with leaders in educational, ministry, civic, and business settings who want to learn how to move beyond conventional topics to explore purpose, meaning, and values in conversation. Whether you are interested in hosting a *bonding conversation* for the purpose of deepening relationships among persons who already know each other or a *bridging conversation* to increase understanding among people of different cultures, faiths, or ways of life, we will collaborate with you to design a conversation, or a series of conversations, that is tailored to your community's needs.

The Journey Conversations Project offers a set of tested resources for cultivating contemplation and compassion in communities. These resources include:

- Journey Conversation Retreats;
- Workshops on the Sacred Art of Conversation;
- Facilitator Training for the Sacred Art of Conversation;
- Customized Conversation Design and Evaluation of Impact;
- Ongoing Coaching and Consultation.

Visit www.journeyconversations.org to learn more about our offerings.

CREDITS

Grateful acknowledgment is given for permission to use the following:

Jeannie E. Roberts, "The Pool," © 2013 by Jeannie E. Roberts, Used by permission.

Jalāl al-Dīn Rumi, "The Guest House," from *The Essential Rumi: New Expanded Edition*, translated by Coleman Barks, with John Moyne, A.J. Arberry, and Reynold Nicholson. New York: HarperOne, 2004. Copyright © Coleman Barks, *The Essential Rumi*.

William Stafford, "Traveling through the Dark," from *The Way It Is: New and Selected Poems*. Copyright © 1988 by the Estate of William Stafford. Reprinted with the permission of The Permissions Company, Inc., on behalf of Graywolf Press, Minneapolis, Minnesota, www.graywolfpress.org.

God In Between Copyright © 1998 Sandy Eisenberg Sasso, with illustrations by Sally Sweetland. Permission granted by Jewish Lights Publishing, Woodstock, Vermont, www.jewishlights.com.

All translations from the Hebrew and Christian Scriptures are from the New Revised Standard Version Bible © 1989, Division of Christian Education of the National Council of the Churches of Christ in the United States of America. Used by permission. All rights reserved.

AVAILABLE FROM BETTER BOOKSTORES. TRY YOUR BOOKSTORE FIRST.

Inspiration

Finding Time for the Timeless: Spirituality in the Workweek
By John McQuiston II
Offers refreshing stories of everyday spiritual practices people use to free themselves from the work and worry mindset of our culture.
5⅛ x 6½, 208 pp, Quality PB, 978-1-59473-383-3 **$9.99**

God the *What*?: What Our Metaphors for God Reveal about Our Beliefs in God *by Carolyn Jane Bohler*
Inspires you to consider a wide range of images of God in order to refine how you imagine God. 6 x 9, 192 pp, Quality PB, 978-1-59473-251-5 **$16.99**

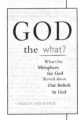

How Did I Get to Be 70 When I'm 35 Inside?: Spiritual Surprises of Later Life *by Linda Douty*
Encourages you to focus on the inner changes of aging to help you greet your later years as the grand adventure they can be. 6 x 9, 208 pp, Quality PB, 978-1-59473-297-3 **$16.99**

Restoring Life's Missing Pieces: The Spiritual Power of Remembering & Reuniting with People, Places, Things & Self *by Caren Goldman*
A powerful and thought-provoking look at reunions of all kinds as roads to remembering and re-membering ourselves.
6 x 9, 208 pp, Quality PB, 978-1-59473-295-9 **$16.99**

Saving Civility: 52 Ways to Tame Rude, Crude & Attitude for a Polite Planet
By Sara Hacala
Provides fifty-two practical ways you can reverse the course of incivility and make the world a more enriching, pleasant place to live.
6 x 9, 240 pp, Quality PB 978-1-59473-314-7 **$16.99**

Spiritually Healthy Divorce: Navigating Disruption with Insight & Hope
by Carolyne Call
A spiritual map to help you move through the twists and turns of divorce.
6 x 9, 224 pp, Quality PB, 978-1-59473-288-1 **$16.99**

Who Is My God? 2nd Edition
An Innovative Guide to Finding Your Spiritual Identity
by the Editors at SkyLight Paths
Provides the Spiritual Identity Self-Test™ to uncover the components of your unique spirituality. 6 x 9, 160 pp, Quality PB, 978-1-59473-014-6 **$15.99**

Journeys of Simplicity
Traveling Light with Thomas Merton, Bashō, Edward Abbey, Annie Dillard & Others
by Philip Harnden
Invites you to consider a more graceful way of traveling through life. PB includes journal pages to help you get started on your own spiritual journey.
5 x 7¼, 144 pp, Quality PB, 978-1-59473-181-5 **$12.99**
5 x 7¼, 128 pp, HC, 978-1-893361-76-8 **$16.95**

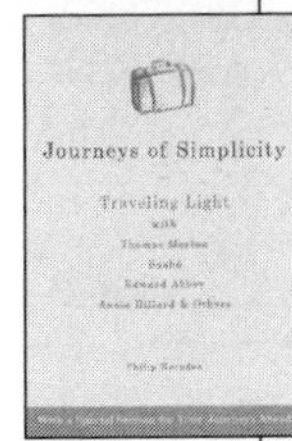

Or phone, fax, mail or e-mail to: SKYLIGHT PATHS **Publishing**
Sunset Farm Offices, Route 4 • P.O. Box 237 • Woodstock, Vermont 05091
Tel: (802) 457-4000 • Fax: (802) 457-4004 • www.skylightpaths.com
Credit card orders: (800) 962-4544 (8:30AM–5:30PM EST Monday–Friday)
Generous discounts on quantity orders. SATISFACTION GUARANTEED. Prices subject to change.

Children's Spirituality

ENDORSED BY CATHOLIC, PROTESTANT, JEWISH, AND BUDDHIST RELIGIOUS LEADERS

Adam & Eve's First Sunset: God's New Day
by Sandy Eisenberg Sasso; Full-color illus. by Joani Keller Rothenberg 9 x 12, 32 pp, Full-color illus., HC, 978-1-58023-177-0 **$17.95*** *For ages 4 & up*

Because Nothing Looks Like God
by Lawrence Kushner and Karen Kushner; Full-color illus. by Dawn W. Majewski
Invites parents and children to explore the questions we all have about God.
11 x 8½, 32 pp, Full-color illus., HC, 978-1-58023-092-6 **$17.99*** *For ages 4 & up*
Also available: **Teacher's Guide** 8½ x 11, 22 pp, PB, 978-1-58023-140-4 **$6.95**

But God Remembered: Stories of Women from Creation to the Promised Land *by Sandy Eisenberg Sasso; Full-color illus. by Bethanne Andersen*
A fascinating collection of four different stories of women only briefly mentioned in biblical tradition and religious texts.
9 x 12, 32 pp, Full-color illus., Quality PB, 978-1-58023-372-9 **$8.99*** *For ages 8 & up*

Cain & Abel: Finding the Fruits of Peace
by Sandy Eisenberg Sasso; Full-color illus. by Joani Keller Rothenberg
A sensitive recasting of the ancient tale shows we have the power to deal with anger in positive ways. "Editor's Choice." —American Library Association's *Booklist*
9 x 12, 32 pp, Full-color illus., HC, 978-1-58023-123-7 **$16.95*** *For ages 5 & up*

Does God Hear My Prayer?
by August Gold; Full-color photos by Diane Hardy Waller
Introduces preschoolers and young readers to prayer and how it helps them express their own emotions.
10 x 8½, 32 pp, Full-color photo illus., Quality PB, 978-1-59473-102-0 **$8.99** *For ages 3–6*

The 11th Commandment: Wisdom from Our Children *by The Children of America*
"If there were an Eleventh Commandment, what would it be?" Children of many religious denominations across America answer this question—in their own drawings and words. "A rare book of spiritual celebration for all people, of all ages, for all time." —*Bookviews* 8 x 10, 48 pp, Full-color illus., HC, 978-1-879045-46-0 **$16.95***
For all ages

For Heaven's Sake *by Sandy Eisenberg Sasso; Full-color illus. by Kathryn Kunz Finney*
Heaven is often found where you least expect it.
9 x 12, 32 pp, Full-color illus., HC, 978-1-58023-054-4 **$16.95*** *For ages 4 & up*

God in Between *by Sandy Eisenberg Sasso; Full-color illus. by Sally Sweetland*
A magical, mythical tale that teaches that God can be found where we are.
9 x 12, 32 pp, Full-color illus., HC, 978-1-879045-86-6 **$16.95*** *For ages 4 & up*

God's Paintbrush: Special 10th Anniversary Edition
by Sandy Eisenberg Sasso; Full-color illus. by Annette Compton
Invites children of all faiths and backgrounds to encounter God through moments in their own lives. 11 x 8½, 32 pp, Full-color illus., HC, 978-1-58023-195-4 **$17.95*** *For ages 4 & up*
Also available: **God's Paintbrush Teacher's Guide**
8½ x 11, 32 pp, PB, 978-1-879045-57-6 **$8.95**

God's Paintbrush Celebration Kit: A Spiritual Activity Kit for Teachers and Students of All Faiths, All Backgrounds 9½ x 12, 40 Full-color Activity Sheets & Teacher Folder w/ complete instructions, HC, 978-1-58023-050-6 **$21.95**
Additional activity sheets available:
8-Student Activity Sheet Pack (40 sheets/5 sessions), 978-1-58023-058-2 **$19.95**
Single-Student Activity Sheet Pack (5 sessions), 978-1-58023-059-9 **$3.95**

I Am God's Paintbrush (A Board Book)
by Sandy Eisenberg Sasso; Full-color illus. by Annette Compton
5 x 5, 24 pp, Full-color illus., Board Book, 978-1-59473-265-2 **$7.99** *For ages 0–4*

* A book from Jewish Lights, SkyLight Paths' sister imprint

Children's Spirituality

ENDORSED BY CATHOLIC, PROTESTANT, JEWISH, AND BUDDHIST RELIGIOUS LEADERS

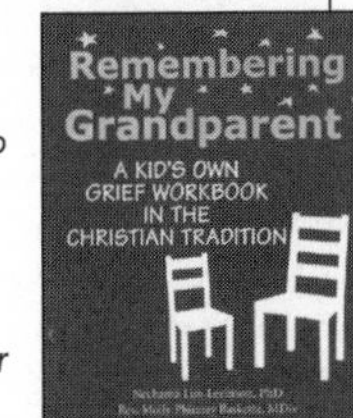

Remembering My Grandparent: A Kid's Own Grief Workbook in the Christian Tradition *by Nechama Liss-Levinson, PhD, and Rev. Molly Phinney Baskette, MDiv* 8 x 10, 48 pp, 2-color text, HC, 978-1-59473-212-6 **$16.99** *For ages 7 & up*

Does God Ever Sleep? *by Joan Sauro, CSJ*
A charming nighttime reminder that God is always present in our lives.
10 x 8½, 32 pp, Full-color photos, Quality PB, 978-1-59473-110-5 **$8.99** *For ages 3–6*

Does God Forgive Me? *by August Gold; Full-color photos by Diane Hardy Waller*
Gently shows how God forgives all that we do if we are truly sorry.
10 x 8½, 32 pp, Full-color photos, Quality PB, 978-1-59473-142-6 **$8.99** *For ages 3–6*

God Said Amen *by Sandy Eisenberg Sasso; Full-color illus. by Avi Katz*
A warm and inspiring tale that shows us that we need only reach out to each other to find the answers to our prayers.
9 x 12, 32 pp, Full-color illus., HC, 978-1-58023-080-3 **$16.95*** *For ages 4 & up*

How Does God Listen? *by Kay Lindahl; Full-color photos by Cynthia Maloney*
How do we know when God is listening to us? Children will find the answers to these questions as they engage their senses while the story unfolds, learning how God listens in the wind, waves, clouds, hot chocolate, perfume, our tears and our laughter.
10 x 8½, 32 pp, Full-color photos, Quality PB, 978-1-59473-084-9 **$8.99** *For ages 3–6*

In God's Hands *by Lawrence Kushner and Gary Schmidt; Full-color illus. by Matthew J. Baek*
9 x 12, 32 pp, Full-color illus., HC, 978-1-58023-224-1 **$16.99*** *For ages 5 & up*

In God's Name *by Sandy Eisenberg Sasso; Full-color illus. by Phoebe Stone*
Like an ancient myth in its poetic text and vibrant illustrations, this award-winning modern fable about the search for God's name celebrates the diversity and, at the same time, the unity of all the people of the world.
9 x 12, 32 pp, Full-color illus., HC, 978-1-879045-26-2 **$16.99*** *For ages 4 & up*

Also available in Spanish: **El nombre de Dios**
9 x 12, 32 pp, Full-color illus., HC, 978-1-893361-63-8 **$16.95**

In Our Image: God's First Creatures
by Nancy Sohn Swartz; Full-color illus. by Melanie Hall
A playful new twist on the Genesis story—from the perspective of the animals. Celebrates the interconnectedness of nature and the harmony of all living things.
9 x 12, 32 pp, Full-color illus., HC, 978-1-879045-99-6 **$16.95*** *For ages 4 & up*

Noah's Wife: The Story of Naamah
by Sandy Eisenberg Sasso; Full-color illus. by Bethanne Andersen
Opens young readers' religious imaginations to new ideas about the well-known story of the Flood. When God tells Noah to bring the animals of the world onto the ark, God also calls on Naamah, Noah's wife, to save each plant on Earth.
9 x 12, 32 pp, Full-color illus., HC, 978-1-58023-134-3 **$16.95*** *For ages 4 & up*

Also available: **Naamah:** Noah's Wife (A Board Book)
by Sandy Eisenberg Sasso; Full-color illus. by Bethanne Andersen
5 x 5, 24 pp, Full-color illus., Board Book, 978-1-893361-56-0 **$7.95** *For ages 0–4*

Where Does God Live? *by August Gold and Matthew J. Perlman*
Helps children and their parents find God in the world around us with simple, practical examples children can relate to.
10 x 8½, 32 pp, Full-color photos, Quality PB, 978-1-893361-39-3 **$8.99** *For ages 3–6*

* A book from Jewish Lights, SkyLight Paths' sister imprint

Children's Spiritual Biography

MULTICULTURAL, NONDENOMINATIONAL, NONSECTARIAN

Ten Amazing People

And How They Changed the World

by Maura D. Shaw; Foreword by Dr. Robert Coles

Full-color illus. by Stephen Marchesi

For ages 7 & up

Shows kids that spiritual people can have an exciting impact on the world around them. Kids will delight in reading about these amazing people and what they accomplished through their words and actions.

Black Elk • Dorothy Day • Malcolm X • Mahatma Gandhi • Martin Luther King, Jr. • Mother Teresa • Janusz Korczak • Desmond Tutu • Thich Nhat Hanh • Albert Schweitzer

"Best Juvenile/Young Adult Non-Fiction Book of the Year."
—*Independent Publisher*

"Will inspire adults and children alike."
—*Globe and Mail* (Toronto)

8½ x 11, 48 pp, Full-color illus., HC, 978-1-893361-47-8 **$17.95** *For ages 7 & up*

Spiritual Biographies for Young People

For Ages 7 & Up

By Maura D. Shaw; Illus. by Stephen Marchesi

6¾ x 8¾, 32 pp, Full-color and b/w illus., HC

Black Elk: Native American Man of Spirit

Through historically accurate illustrations and photos, inspiring age-appropriate activities and Black Elk's own words, this colorful biography introduces children to a remarkable person who ensured that the traditions and beliefs of his people would not be forgotten.

978-1-59473-043-6 **$12.99**

Dorothy Day: A Catholic Life of Action

Introduces children to one of the most inspiring women of the twentieth century, a down-to-earth spiritual leader who saw the presence of God in every person she met. Includes practical activities, a timeline and a list of important words to know.

978-1-59473-011-5 **$12.99**

Gandhi: India's Great Soul

The only biography of Gandhi that balances a simple text with illustrations, photos and activities that encourage children and adults to talk about how to make changes happen without violence. Introduces children to important concepts of freedom, equality and justice among people of all backgrounds and religions.

978-1-893361-91-1 **$12.95**

Thich Nhat Hanh: Buddhism in Action

Warm illustrations, photos, age-appropriate activities and Thich Nhat Hanh's own poems introduce a great man to children in a way they can understand and enjoy. Includes a list of important Buddhist words to know.

978-1-893361-87-4 **$12.95**

Spirituality of the Seasons

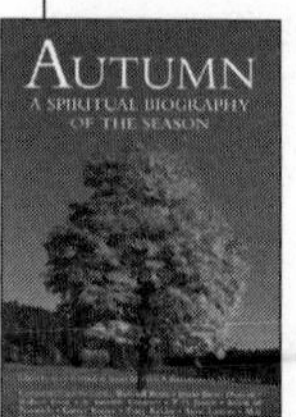

Autumn: A Spiritual Biography of the Season
Edited by Gary Schmidt and Susan M. Felch; Illus. by Mary Azarian
Rejoice in autumn as a time of preparation and reflection. Includes Wendell Berry, David James Duncan, Robert Frost, A. Bartlett Giamatti, E. B. White, P. D. James, Julian of Norwich, Garret Keizer, Tracy Kidder, Anne Lamott, May Sarton.
6 x 9, 320 pp, b/w illus., Quality PB, 978-1-59473-118-1 **$18.99**

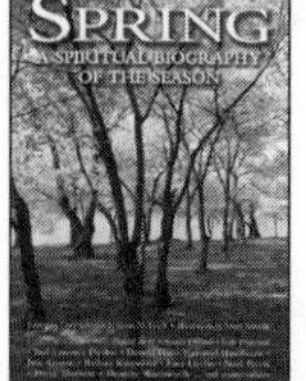

Spring: A Spiritual Biography of the Season
Edited by Gary Schmidt and Susan M. Felch; Illus. by Mary Azarian
Explore the gentle unfurling of spring and reflect on how nature celebrates rebirth and renewal. Includes Jane Kenyon, Lucy Larcom, Harry Thurston, Nathaniel Hawthorne, Noel Perrin, Annie Dillard, Martha Ballard, Barbara Kingsolver, Dorothy Wordsworth, Donald Hall, David Brill, Lionel Basney, Isak Dinesen, Paul Laurence Dunbar. 6 x 9, 352 pp, b/w illus., Quality PB, 978-1-59473-246-1 **$18.99**

Summer: A Spiritual Biography of the Season
Edited by Gary Schmidt and Susan M. Felch; Illus. by Barry Moser
"A sumptuous banquet.... These selections lift up an exquisite wholeness found within an everyday sophistication." — ★ *Publishers Weekly* starred review
Includes Anne Lamott, Luci Shaw, Ray Bradbury, Richard Selzer, Thomas Lynch, Walt Whitman, Carl Sandburg, Sherman Alexie, Madeleine L'Engle, Jamaica Kincaid.
6 x 9, 304 pp, b/w illus., Quality PB, 978-1-59473-183-9 **$18.99**
HC, 978-1-59473-083-2 **$21.99**

Winter: A Spiritual Biography of the Season
Edited by Gary Schmidt and Susan M. Felch; Illus. by Barry Moser
"This outstanding anthology features top-flight nature and spirituality writers on the fierce, inexorable season of winter.... Remarkably lively and warm, despite the icy subject." — ★ *Publishers Weekly* starred review
Includes Will Campbell, Rachel Carson, Annie Dillard, Donald Hall, Ron Hansen, Jane Kenyon, Jamaica Kincaid, Barry Lopez, Kathleen Norris, John Updike, E. B. White.
6 x 9, 288 pp, b/w illus., Deluxe PB w/ flaps, 978-1-893361-92-8 **$18.95**
HC, 978-1-893361-53-9 **$21.95**

Spirituality / Animal Companions

Blessing the Animals: Prayers and Ceremonies to Celebrate God's Creatures, Wild and Tame *Edited and with Introductions by Lynn L. Caruso*
5¼ x 7¼, 256 pp, Quality PB, 978-1-59473-253-9 **$15.99**; HC, 978-1-59473-145-7 **$19.99**

Remembering My Pet: A Kid's Own Spiritual Workbook for When a Pet Dies
by Nechama Liss-Levinson, PhD, and Rev. Molly Phinney Baskette, MDiv; Foreword by Lynn L. Caruso
8 x 10, 48 pp, 2-color text, HC, 978-1-59473-221-8 **$16.99**

What Animals Can Teach Us about Spirituality: Inspiring Lessons from Wild and Tame Creatures *by Diana L. Guerrero* 6 x 9, 176 pp, Quality PB, 978-1-893361-84-3 **$16.95**

Spirituality—A Week Inside

Lighting the Lamp of Wisdom: A Week Inside a Yoga Ashram
by John Ittner; Foreword by Dr. David Frawley
6 x 9, 192 pp, b/w photos, Quality PB, 978-1-893361-52-2 **$15.95**

Making a Heart for God: A Week Inside a Catholic Monastery
by Dianne Aprile; Foreword by Brother Patrick Hart, OCSO
6 x 9, 224 pp, b/w photos, Quality PB, 978-1-893361-49-2 **$16.95**

Waking Up: A Week Inside a Zen Monastery
by Jack Maguire; Foreword by John Daido Loori, Roshi
6 x 9, 224 pp, b/w photos, Quality PB, 978-1-893361-55-3 **$16.95**; HC, 978-1-893361-13-3 **$21.95**

Spiritual Poetry—The Mystic Poets

Experience these mystic poets as you never have before. Each beautiful, compact book includes a brief introduction to the poet's time and place, a summary of the major themes of the poet's mysticism and religious tradition, essential selections from the poet's most important works, and an appreciative preface by a contemporary spiritual writer.

Hafiz

The Mystic Poets

Translated and with Notes by Gertrude Bell

Preface by Ibrahim Gamard

Hafiz is known throughout the world as Persia's greatest poet, with sales of his poems in Iran today only surpassed by those of the Qur'an itself. His probing and joyful verse speaks to people from all backgrounds who long to taste and feel divine love and experience harmony with all living things.

5 x 7¼, 144 pp, HC, 978-1-59473-009-2 **$16.99**

Hopkins

The Mystic Poets

Preface by Rev. Thomas Ryan, CSP

Gerard Manley Hopkins, Christian mystical poet, is beloved for his use of fresh language and startling metaphors to describe the world around him. Although his verse is lovely, beneath the surface lies a searching soul, wrestling with and yearning for God.

5 x 7¼, 112 pp, HC, 978-1-59473-010-8 **$16.99**

Tagore

The Mystic Poets

Preface by Swami Adiswarananda

Rabindranath Tagore is often considered the Shakespeare of modern India. A great mystic, Tagore was the teacher of W. B. Yeats and Robert Frost, the close friend of Albert Einstein and Mahatma Gandhi, and the winner of the Nobel Prize for Literature. This beautiful sampling of Tagore's two most important works, *The Gardener* and *Gitanjali*, offers a glimpse into his spiritual vision that has inspired people around the world.

5 x 7¼, 144 pp, HC, 978-1-59473-008-5 **$16.99**

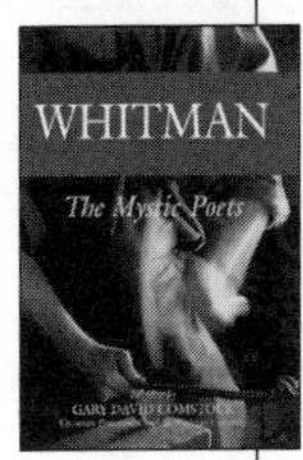

Whitman

The Mystic Poets

Preface by Gary David Comstock

Walt Whitman was the most innovative and influential poet of the nineteenth century. This beautiful sampling of Whitman's most important poetry from *Leaves of Grass*, and selections from his prose writings, offers a glimpse into the spiritual side of his most radical themes—love for country, love for others and love of self.

5 x 7¼, 192 pp, HC, 978-1-59473-041-2 **$16.99**

Bible Stories / Folktales

Abraham's Bind & Other Bible Tales of Trickery, Folly, Mercy and Love *by Michael J. Caduto*
New retellings of episodes in the lives of familiar biblical characters explore relevant life lessons. 6 x 9, 224 pp, HC, 978-1-59473-186-0 **$19.99**

Daughters of the Desert: Stories of Remarkable Women from Christian, Jewish and Muslim Traditions *by Claire Rudolf Murphy, Meghan Nuttall Sayres, Mary Cronk Farrell, Sarah Conover and Betsy Wharton*
Breathes new life into the old tales of our female ancestors in faith. Uses traditional scriptural passages as starting points, then with vivid detail fills in historical context and place. Chapters reveal the voices of Sarah, Hagar, Huldah, Esther, Salome, Mary Magdalene, Lydia, Khadija, Fatima and many more. Historical fiction ideal for readers of all ages.
5½ x 8½, 192 pp, Quality PB, 978-1-59473-106-8 **$14.99** Inc. reader's discussion guide
HC, 978-1-893361-72-0 **$19.95**

The Triumph of Eve & Other Subversive Bible Tales
by Matt Biers-Ariel
These engaging retellings of familiar Bible stories are witty, often hilarious and always profound. They invite you to grapple with questions and issues that are often hidden in the original texts.
5½ x 8½, 192 pp, Quality PB, 978-1-59473-176-1 **$14.99**

Also available: **The Triumph of Eve Teacher's Guide**
8½ x 11, 44 pp, PB, 978-1-59473-152-5 **$8.99**

Wisdom in the Telling
Finding Inspiration and Grace in Traditional Folktales and Myths Retold
by Lorraine Hartin-Gelardi
6 x 9, 192 pp, HC, 978-1-59473-185-3 **$19.99**

Religious Etiquette / Reference

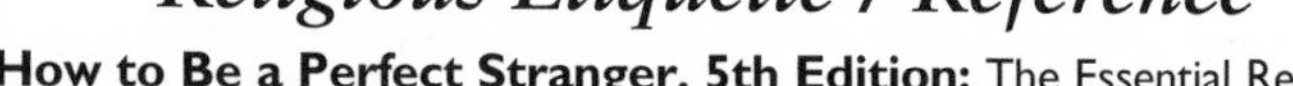

How to Be a Perfect Stranger, 5th Edition: The Essential Religious Etiquette Handbook *Edited by Stuart M. Matlins and Arthur J. Magida*
The indispensable guidebook to help the well-meaning guest when visiting other people's religious ceremonies. A straightforward guide to the rituals and celebrations of the major religions and denominations in the United States and Canada from the perspective of an interested guest of any other faith, based on information obtained from authorities of each religion. Belongs in every living room, library and office. Covers:

African American Methodist Churches • Assemblies of God • Bahá'í Faith • Baptist • Buddhist • Christian Church (Disciples of Christ) • Christian Science (Church of Christ, Scientist) • Churches of Christ • Episcopalian and Anglican • Hindu • Islam • Jehovah's Witnesses • Jewish • Lutheran • Mennonite/Amish • Methodist • Mormon (Church of Jesus Christ of Latter-day Saints) • Native American/First Nations • Orthodox Churches • Pentecostal Church of God • Presbyterian • Quaker (Religious Society of Friends) • Reformed Church in America/Canada • Roman Catholic • Seventh-day Adventist • Sikh • Unitarian Universalist • United Church of Canada • United Church of Christ

"The things Miss Manners forgot to tell us about religion."

—*Los Angeles Times*

"Finally, for those inclined to undertake their own spiritual journeys … tells visitors what to expect." —*New York Times*

6 x 9, 432 pp, Quality PB, 978-1-59473-294-2 **$19.99**

The Perfect Stranger's Guide to Funerals and Grieving Practices: A Guide to Etiquette in Other People's Religious Ceremonies *Edited by Stuart M. Matlins*
6 x 9, 240 pp, Quality PB, 978-1-893361-20-1 **$16.95**

The Perfect Stranger's Guide to Wedding Ceremonies: A Guide to Etiquette in Other People's Religious Ceremonies *Edited by Stuart M. Matlins*
6 x 9, 208 pp, Quality PB, 978-1-893361-19-5 **$16.95**

Professional Spiritual & Pastoral Care Resources

Professional Spiritual & Pastoral Care
A Practical Clergy and Chaplain's Handbook
Edited by Rabbi Stephen B. Roberts, MBA, MHL, BCJC
An essential resource integrating the classic foundations of pastoral care with the latest approaches to spiritual care, specifically intended for professionals who work or spend time with congregants in acute care hospitals, behavioral health facilities, rehabilitation centers and long-term care facilities.
6 x 9, 480 pp, HC, 978-1-59473-312-3 **$50.00**

Disaster Spiritual Care
Practical Clergy Responses to Community, Regional and National Tragedy
Edited by Rabbi Stephen B. Roberts, BCJC, and Rev. Willard W.C. Ashley, Sr., DMin, DH
The definitive guidebook for counseling not only the victims of disaster but also the clergy and caregivers who are called to service in the wake of crisis.
6 x 9, 384 pp, HC, 978-1-59473-240-9 **$50.00**

Learning to Lead
Lessons in Leadership for People of Faith
Edited by Rev. Williard W.C. Ashley Sr., MDiv, DMin, DH
In this multifaith, cross-cultural and comprehensive resource for both clergy and lay persons, contributors who are experts in the field explore how to engage spiritual leaders and teach them how to bring healing, faith, justice and support to communities and congregations.
6 x 9, 384 pp, HC, 978-1-59473-432-8 **$40.00**

How to Be a Perfect Stranger, 5th Edition
The Essential Religious Etiquette Handbook
Edited by Stuart M. Matlins and Arthur J. Magida
The indispensable guidebook to help the well-meaning guest when visiting other people's religious ceremonies. A straightforward guide to the rituals and celebrations of the major religions and denominations in the United States and Canada from the perspective of an interested guest of any other faith, based on information obtained from authorities of each religion. Belongs in every living room, library and office. Covers:
African American Methodist Churches • Assemblies of God • Bahá'í Faith • Baptist • Buddhist • Christian Church (Disciples of Christ) • Christian Science (Church of Christ, Scientist) • Churches of Christ • Episcopalian and Anglican • Hindu • Islam • Jehovah's Witnesses • Jewish • Lutheran • Mennonite/Amish • Methodist • Mormon (Church of Jesus Christ of Latter-day Saints) • Native American/First Nations • Orthodox Churches • Pentecostal Church of God • Presbyterian • Quaker (Religious Society of Friends) • Reformed Church in America/Canada • Roman Catholic • Seventh-day Adventist • Sikh • Unitarian Universalist • United Church of Canada • United Church of Christ

"The things Miss Manners forgot to tell us about religion."
—*Los Angeles Times*

6 x 9, 432 pp, Quality PB, 978-1-59473-294-2 **$19.99**

The Perfect Stranger's Guide to Funerals and Grieving Practices
A Guide to Etiquette in Other People's Religious Ceremonies
Edited by Stuart M. Matlins
6 x 9, 240 pp, Quality PB, 978-1-893361-20-1 **$16.95**

Jewish Pastoral Care, 2nd Edition
A Practical Handbook from Traditional & Contemporary Sources
Edited by Rabbi Dayle A. Friedman, MSW, MAJCS, BCC
6 x 9, 528 pp, Quality PB, 978-1-58023-427-6 **$30.00**
(A book from Jewish Lights, SkyLight Paths' sister imprint)

Caresharing: A Reciprocal Approach to Caregiving and Care Receiving in the Complexities of Aging, Illness or Disability
by Marty Richards
6 x 9, 256 pp, Quality PB, 978-1-59473-286-7 **$16.99**; HC, 978-1-59473-247-8 **$24.99**

InterActive Faith
The Essential Interreligious Community-Building Handbook
Edited by Rev. Bud Heckman with Rori Picker Neiss
6 x 9, 304 pp, Quality PB, 978-1-59473-273-7 **$16.99**; HC, 978-1-59473-237-9 **$29.99**

Judaism / Christianity / Islam / Interfaith

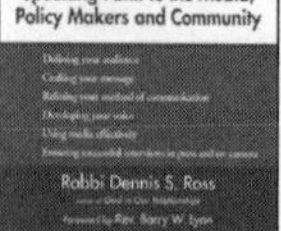

All Politics Is Religious: Speaking Faith to the Media, Policy Makers and Community *By Rabbi Dennis S. Ross; Foreword by Rev. Barry W. Lynn*
Provides ideas and strategies for expressing a clear, forceful and progressive religious point of view that is all too often overlooked and under-represented in public discourse. 6 x 9, 192 pp, Quality PB, 978-1-59473-374-1 **$18.99**

Religion Gone Astray: What We Found at the Heart of Interfaith
By Pastor Don Mackenzie, Rabbi Ted Falcon and Imam Jamal Rahman
Welcome to the deeper dimensions of interfaith dialogue—exploring that which divides us personally, spiritually and institutionally.
6 x 9, 192 pp, Quality PB, 978-1-59473-317-8 **$16.99**

Getting to the Heart of Interfaith: The Eye-Opening, Hope-Filled Friendship of a Pastor, a Rabbi & an Imam *by Pastor Don Mackenzie, Rabbi Ted Falcon and Imam Jamal Rahman*
6 x 9, 192 pp, Quality PB, 978-1-59473-263-8 **$16.99**

Hearing the Call across Traditions: Readings on Faith and Service
Edited by Adam Davis; Foreword by Eboo Patel
6 x 9, 352 pp, Quality PB, 978-1-59473-303-1 **$18.99**; HC, 978-1-59473-264-5 **$29.99**

How to Do Good & Avoid Evil: A Global Ethic from the Sources of Judaism
by Hans Küng and Rabbi Walter Homolka; Translated by Rev. Dr. John Bowden
6 x 9, 224 pp, HC, 978-1-59473-255-3 **$19.99**

Blessed Relief: What Christians Can Learn from Buddhists about Suffering
by Gordon Peerman 6 x 9, 208 pp, Quality PB, 978-1-59473-252-2 **$16.99**

Christians & Jews—Faith to Faith: Tragic History, Promising Present, Fragile Future *by Rabbi James Rudin* 6 x 9, 288 pp, HC, 978-1-58023-432-0 **$24.99***

Christians & Jews in Dialogue: Learning in the Presence of the Other *by Mary C. Boys and Sara S. Lee; Foreword by Dorothy C. Bass* 6 x 9, 240 pp, Quality PB, 978-1-59473-254-6 **$18.99**

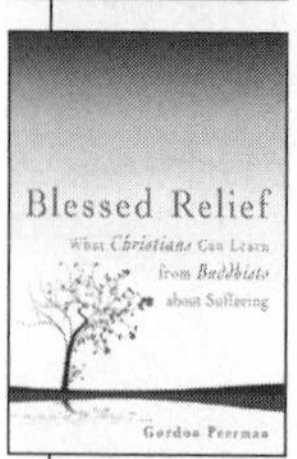

InterActive Faith: The Essential Interreligious Community-Building Handbook
Edited by Rev. Bud Heckman with Rori Picker Neiss; Foreword by Rev. Dirk Ficca
6 x 9, 304 pp, Quality PB, 978-1-59473-273-7 **$16.99**; HC, 978-1-59473-237-9 **$29.99**

The Jewish Approach to God: A Brief Introduction for Christians
by Rabbi Neil Gillman, PhD 5½ x 8½, 192 pp, Quality PB, 978-1-58023-190-9 **$16.95***

The Jewish Approach to Repairing the World (*Tikkun Olam*): A Brief Introduction for Christians *by Rabbi Elliot N. Dorff, PhD, with Rev. Cory Willson*
5½ x 8½, 256 pp, Quality PB, 978-1-58023-349-1 **$16.99***

The Jewish Connection to Israel, the Promised Land: A Brief Introduction for Christians *by Rabbi Eugene Korn, PhD* 5½ x 8½, 192 pp, Quality PB, 978-1-58023-318-7 **$14.99***

Jewish Holidays: A Brief Introduction for Christians *by Rabbi Kerry M. Olitzky and Rabbi Daniel Judson* 5½ x 8½, 176 pp, Quality PB, 978-1-58023-302-6 **$16.99***

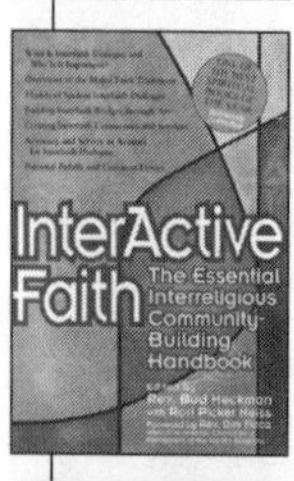

Jewish Ritual: A Brief Introduction for Christians
by Rabbi Kerry M. Olitzky and Rabbi Daniel Judson 5½ x 8½, 144 pp, Quality PB, 978-1-58023-210-4 **$14.99***

Jewish Spirituality: A Brief Introduction for Christians *by Rabbi Lawrence Kushner*
5½ x 8½, 112 pp, Quality PB, 978-1-58023-150-3 **$12.95***

A Jewish Understanding of the New Testament *by Rabbi Samuel Sandmel; New preface by Rabbi David Sandmel* 5½ x 8½, 368 pp, Quality PB, 978-1-59473-048-1 **$19.99***

Modern Jews Engage the New Testament: Enhancing Jewish Well-Being in a Christian Environment *by Rabbi Michael J. Cook, PhD* 6 x 9, 416 pp, HC, 978-1-58023-313-2 **$29.99***

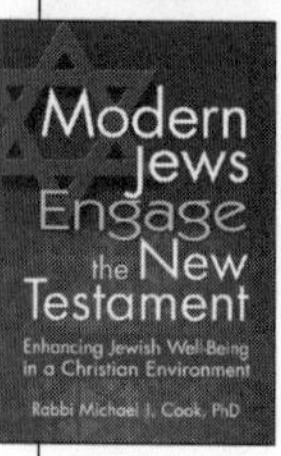

Talking about God: Exploring the Meaning of Religious Life with Kierkegaard, Buber, Tillich and Heschel *by Daniel F. Polish, PhD* 6 x 9, 160 pp, Quality PB, 978-1-59473-272-0 **$16.99**

We Jews and Jesus: Exploring Theological Differences for Mutual Understanding
by Rabbi Samuel Sandmel; New preface by Rabbi David Sandmel
6 x 9, 192 pp, Quality PB, 978-1-59473-208-9 **$16.99**

Who Are the *Real* Chosen People? The Meaning of Chosenness in Judaism, Christianity and Islam *by Reuven Firestone, PhD*
6 x 9, 176 pp, Quality PB, 978-1-59473-290-4 **$16.99**; HC, 978-1-59473-248-5 **$21.99**

* A book from Jewish Lights, SkyLight Paths' sister imprint

Prayer / Meditation

Men Pray: Voices of Strength, Faith, Healing, Hope and Courage
Created by the Editors at SkyLight Paths
Celebrates the rich variety of ways men around the world have called out to the Divine—with words of joy, praise, gratitude, wonder, petition and even anger—from the ancient world up to our own day.
5 x 7¼, 192 pp, HC, 978-1-59473-395-6 **$16.99**

Sacred Attention: A Spiritual Practice for Finding God in the Moment
by Margaret D. McGee
Framed on the Christian liturgical year, this inspiring guide explores ways to develop a practice of attention as a means of talking—and listening—to God.
6 x 9, 144 pp, Quality PB, 978-1-59473-291-1 **$16.99**

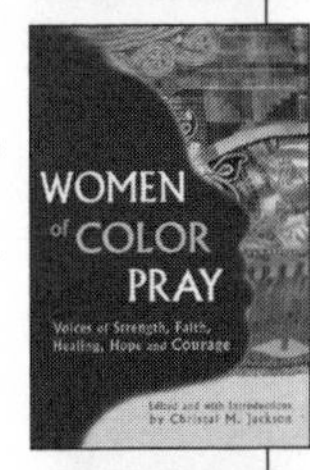

Women of Color Pray: Voices of Strength, Faith, Healing, Hope and Courage
Edited and with Introductions by Christal M. Jackson
Through these prayers, poetry, lyrics, meditations and affirmations, you will share in the strong and undeniable connection women of color share with God.
5 x 7¼, 208 pp, Quality PB, 978-1-59473-077-1 **$15.99**

The Art of Public Prayer, 2nd Edition: Not for Clergy Only
by Lawrence A. Hoffman, PhD 6 x 9, 288 pp, Quality PB, 978-1-893361-06-5 **$19.99**

A Heart of Stillness: A Complete Guide to Learning the Art of Meditation
by David A. Cooper 5½ x 8½, 272 pp, Quality PB, 978-1-893361-03-4 **$18.99**

Living into Hope: A Call to Spiritual Action for Such a Time as This
by Rev. Dr. Joan Brown Campbell; Foreword by Karen Armstrong
6 x 9, 208 pp, HC, 978-1-59473-283-6 **$21.99**

Meditation without Gurus: A Guide to the Heart of Practice
by Clark Strand 5½ x 8½, 192 pp, Quality PB, 978-1-893361-93-5 **$16.95**

Prayers to an Evolutionary God
by William Cleary; Afterword by Diarmuid O'Murchu
6 x 9, 208 pp, HC, 978-1-59473-006-1 **$21.99**

Praying with Our Hands: 21 Practices of Embodied Prayer from the World's Spiritual Traditions *by Jon M. Sweeney; Photos by Jennifer J. Wilson; Foreword by Mother Tessa Bielecki; Afterword by Taitetsu Unno, PhD*
8 x 8, 96 pp, 22 duotone photos, Quality PB, 978-1-893361-16-4 **$16.95**

Secrets of Prayer: A Multifaith Guide to Creating Personal Prayer in Your Life
by Nancy Corcoran, CSJ
6 x 9, 160 pp, Quality PB, 978-1-59473-215-7 **$16.99**

Three Gates to Meditation Practice: A Personal Journey into Sufism, Buddhism, and Judaism *by David A. Cooper* 5½ x 8½, 240 pp, Quality PB, 978-1-893361-22-5 **$16.95**

Prayer / M. Basil Pennington, OCSO

Finding Grace at the Center, 3rd Edition: The Beginning of Centering Prayer *with Thomas Keating, OCSO, and Thomas E. Clarke, SJ; Foreword by Rev. Cynthia Bourgeault, PhD* A practical guide to a simple and beautiful form of meditative prayer. 5 x 7¼,128 pp, Quality PB, 978-1-59473-182-2 **$12.99**

The Monks of Mount Athos: A Western Monk's Extraordinary Spiritual Journey on Eastern Holy Ground *Foreword by Archimandrite Dionysios*
Explores the landscape, monastic communities and food of Athos.
6 x 9, 352 pp, Quality PB, 978-1-893361-78-2 **$18.95**

Psalms: A Spiritual Commentary *Illus. by Phillip Ratner*
Reflections on some of the most beloved passages from the Bible's most widely read book. 6 x 9, 176 pp, 24 full-page b/w illus., Quality PB, 978-1-59473-234-8 **$16.99**

The Song of Songs: A Spiritual Commentary *Illus. by Phillip Ratner*
Explore the Bible's most challenging mystical text.
6 x 9, 160 pp, 14 full-page b/w illus., Quality PB, 978-1-59473-235-5 **$16.99**
HC, 978-1-59473-004-7 **$19.99**

Women's Interest

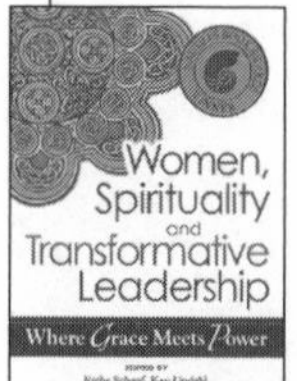

Women, Spirituality and Transformative Leadership
Where Grace Meets Power
Edited by Kathe Schaaf, Kay Lindahl, Kathleen S. Hurty, PhD, and Reverend Guo Cheen
A dynamic conversation on the power of women's spiritual leadership and its emerging patterns of transformation. 6 x 9, 288 pp, Hardcover, 978-1-59473-313-0 **$24.99**

Spiritually Healthy Divorce: Navigating Disruption with Insight & Hope
by Carolyne Call A spiritual map to help you move through the twists and turns of divorce. 6 x 9, 224 pp, Quality PB, 978-1-59473-288-1 **$16.99**

New Feminist Christianity: Many Voices, Many Views
Edited by Mary E. Hunt and Diann L. Neu
Insights from ministers and theologians, activists and leaders, artists and liturgists who are shaping the future. Taken together, their voices offer a starting point for building new models of religious life and worship.
6 x 9, 384 pp, HC, 978-1-59473-285-0 **$24.99**

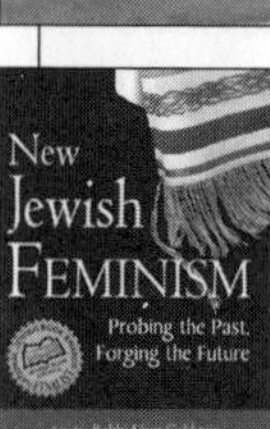

New Jewish Feminism: Probing the Past, Forging the Future
Edited by Rabbi Elyse Goldstein; Foreword by Anita Diamant
Looks at the growth and accomplishments of Jewish feminism and what they mean for Jewish women today and tomorrow. Features the voices of women from every area of Jewish life, addressing the important issues that concern Jewish women.
6 x 9, 480 pp, Quality PB, 978-1-58023-448-1 **$19.99**; HC, 978-1-58023-359-0 **$24.99***

Bread, Body, Spirit: Finding the Sacred in Food
Edited and with Introductions by Alice Peck 6 x 9, 224 pp, Quality PB, 978-1-59473-242-3 **$19.99**

Dance—The Sacred Art: The Joy of Movement as a Spiritual Practice
by Cynthia Winton-Henry 5½ x 8½, 224 pp, Quality PB, 978-1-59473-268-3 **$16.99**

Daughters of the Desert: Stories of Remarkable Women from Christian, Jewish and Muslim Traditions
by Claire Rudolf Murphy, Meghan Nuttall Sayres, Mary Cronk Farrell, Sarah Conover and Betsy Wharton
5½ x 8½, 192 pp, Illus., Quality PB, 978-1-59473-106-8 **$14.99** Inc. reader's discussion guide

The Divine Feminine in Biblical Wisdom Literature
Selections Annotated & Explained
Translation & Annotation by Rabbi Rami Shapiro; Foreword by Rev. Cynthia Bourgeault, PhD
5½ x 8½, 240 pp, Quality PB, 978-1-59473-109-9 **$16.99**

Divining the Body: Reclaim the Holiness of Your Physical Self
by Jan Phillips 8 x 8, 256 pp, Quality PB, 978-1-59473-080-1 **$18.99**

Honoring Motherhood: Prayers, Ceremonies & Blessings
Edited and with Introductions by Lynn L. Caruso
5 x 7¼, 272 pp, Quality PB, 978-1-58473-384-0 **$9.99**; HC, 978-1-59473-239-3 **$19.99**

Next to Godliness: Finding the Sacred in Housekeeping
Edited by Alice Peck 6 x 9, 224 pp, Quality PB, 978-1-59473-214-0 **$19.99**

ReVisions: Seeing Torah through a Feminist Lens
by Rabbi Elyse Goldstein 5½ x 8½, 224 pp, Quality PB, 978-1-58023-117-6 **$16.95***

The Triumph of Eve & Other Subversive Bible Tales
by Matt Biers-Ariel 5½ x 8½, 192 pp, Quality PB, 978-1-59473-176-1 **$14.99**

White Fire: A Portrait of Women Spiritual Leaders in America
by Malka Drucker; Photos by Gay Block 7 x 10, 320 pp, b/w photos, HC, 978-1-893361-64-5 **$24.95**

Woman Spirit Awakening in Nature: Growing Into the Fullness of Who You Are
by Nancy Barrett Chickerneo, PhD; Foreword by Eileen Fisher
8 x 8, 224 pp, b/w illus., Quality PB, 978-1-59473-250-8 **$16.99**

Women of Color Pray: Voices of Strength, Faith, Healing, Hope and Courage
Edited and with Introductions by Christal M. Jackson
5 x 7¼, 208 pp, Quality PB, 978-1-59473-077-1 **$15.99**

The Women's Torah Commentary: New Insights from Women Rabbis on the 54 Weekly Torah Portions *Edited by Rabbi Elyse Goldstein*
6 x 9, 496 pp, Quality PB, 978-1-58023-370-5 **$19.99**; HC, 978-1-58023-076-6 **$34.95***

* A book from Jewish Lights, SkyLight Paths' sister imprint

Spirituality & Crafts

Beading—The Creative Spirit: Finding Your Sacred Center through the Art of Beadwork *by Rev. Wendy Ellsworth*
Invites you on a spiritual pilgrimage into the kaleidoscope world of glass and color. 7 x 9, 240 pp, 8-page color insert, 40+ b/w photos and 40 diagrams, Quality PB, 978-1-59473-267-6 **$18.99**

Contemplative Crochet: A Hands-On Guide for Interlocking Faith and Craft *by Cindy Crandall-Frazier; Foreword by Linda Skolnik*
Illuminates the spiritual lessons you can learn through crocheting.
7 x 9, 208 pp, b/w photos, Quality PB, 978-1-59473-238-6 **$16.99**

The Knitting Way: A Guide to Spiritual Self-Discovery
by Linda Skolnik and Janice MacDaniels Examines how you can explore and strengthen your spiritual life through knitting.
7 x 9, 240 pp, b/w photos, Quality PB, 978-1-59473-079-5 **$16.99**

The Painting Path: Embodying Spiritual Discovery through Yoga, Brush and Color *by Linda Novick; Foreword by Richard Segalman*
Explores the divine connection you can experience through art.
7 x 9, 208 pp, 8-page color insert, plus b/w photos, Quality PB, 978-1-59473-226-3 **$18.99**

The Quilting Path: A Guide to Spiritual Discovery through Fabric, Thread and Kabbalah *by Louise Silk*
Explores how to cultivate personal growth through quilt making.
7 x 9, 192 pp, b/w photos and illus., Quality PB, 978-1-59473-206-5 **$16.99**

The Scrapbooking Journey: A Hands-On Guide to Spiritual Discovery
by Cory Richardson-Lauve; Foreword by Stacy Julian Reveals how this craft can become a practice used to deepen and shape your life.
7 x 9, 176 pp, 8-page color insert, plus b/w photos, Quality PB, 978-1-59473-216-4 **$18.99**

The Soulwork of Clay: A Hands-On Approach to Spirituality
by Marjory Zoet Bankson; Photos by Peter Bankson
Takes you through the seven-step process of making clay into a pot, drawing parallels at each stage to the process of spiritual growth.
7 x 9, 192 pp, b/w photos, Quality PB, 978-1-59473-249-2 **$16.99**

Kabbalah / Enneagram

(Books from Jewish Lights Publishing, SkyLight Paths' sister imprint)

Cast in God's Image: Discover Your Personality Type Using the Enneagram and Kabbalah *by Rabbi Howard A. Addison, PhD* 7 x 9, 176 pp, Quality PB, 978-1-58023-124-4 **$16.95**

Ehyeh: A Kabbalah for Tomorrow *by Rabbi Arthur Green, PhD*
6 x 9, 224 pp, Quality PB, 978-1-58023-213-5 **$18.99**

The Enneagram and Kabbalah, 2nd Edition: Reading Your Soul
by Rabbi Howard A. Addison, PhD 6 x 9, 192 pp, Quality PB, 978-1-58023-229-6 **$16.99**

The Gift of Kabbalah: Discovering the Secrets of Heaven, Renewing Your Life on Earth *by Tamar Frankiel, PhD* 6 x 9, 256 pp, Quality PB, 978-1-58023-141-1 **$16.95**

God in Your Body: Kabbalah, Mindfulness and Embodied Spiritual Practice
by Jay Michaelson 6 x 9, 272 pp, Quality PB, 978-1-58023-304-0 **$18.99**

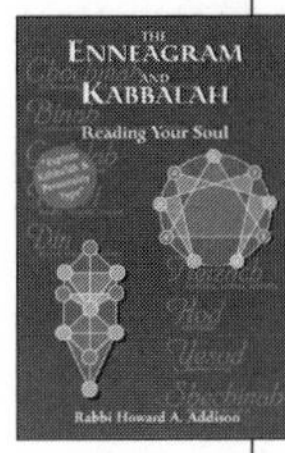

Jewish Mysticism and the Spiritual Life: Classical Texts, Contemporary Reflections
Edited by Dr. Lawrence Fine, Dr. Eitan Fishbane and Rabbi Or N. Rose
6 x 9, 256 pp, HC, 978-1-58023-434-4 **$24.99**

Kabbalah: A Brief Introduction for Christians
by Tamar Frankiel, PhD 5½ x 8½, 208 pp, Quality PB, 978-1-58023-303-3 **$16.99**

Zohar: Annotated & Explained *Translation & Annotation by Daniel C. Matt; Foreword by Andrew Harvey* 5½ x 8½, 176 pp, Quality PB, 978-1-893361-51-5 **$15.99**

Spirituality

Gathering at God's Table: The Meaning of Mission in the Feast of Faith
By Katharine Jefferts Schori
A profound reminder of our role in the larger frame of God's dream for a restored and reconciled world. 6 x 9, 256 pp, HC, 978-1-59473-316-1 **$21.99**

The Heartbeat of God: Finding the Sacred in the Middle of Everything
by Katharine Jefferts Schori; Foreword by Joan Chittister, OSB
Explores our connections to other people, to other nations and with the environment through the lens of faith. 6 x 9, 240 pp, HC, 978-1-59473-292-8 **$21.99**

A Dangerous Dozen: Twelve Christians Who Threatened the Status Quo but Taught Us to Live Like Jesus
by the Rev. Canon C. K. Robertson, PhD; Foreword by Archbishop Desmond Tutu
Profiles twelve visionary men and women who challenged society and showed the world a different way of living. 6 x 9, 208 pp, Quality PB, 978-1-59473-298-0 **$16.99**

Decision Making & Spiritual Discernment: The Sacred Art of Finding Your Way *by Nancy L. Bieber*
Presents three essential aspects of Spirit-led decision making: willingness, attentiveness and responsiveness. 5½ x 8½, 208 pp, Quality PB, 978-1-59473-289-8 **$16.99**

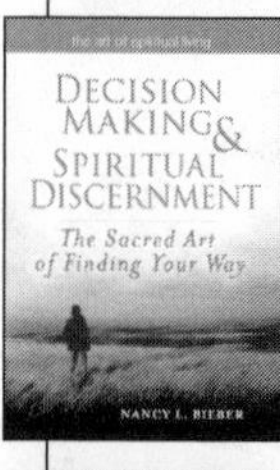

Laugh Your Way to Grace: Reclaiming the Spiritual Power of Humor
by Rev. Susan Sparks A powerful, humorous case for laughter as a spiritual, healing path. 6 x 9, 176 pp, Quality PB, 978-1-59473-280-5 **$16.99**

Bread, Body, Spirit: Finding the Sacred in Food
Edited and with Introductions by Alice Peck 6 x 9, 224 pp, Quality PB, 978-1-59473-242-3 **$19.99**

Claiming Earth as Common Ground: The Ecological Crisis through the Lens of Faith
by Andrea Cohen-Kiener; Foreword by Rev. Sally Bingham
6 x 9, 192 pp, Quality PB, 978-1-59473-261-4 **$16.99**

Creating a Spiritual Retirement: A Guide to the Unseen Possibilities in Our Lives
by Molly Srode 6 x 9, 208 pp, b/w photos, Quality PB, 978-1-59473-050-4 **$14.99**

Creative Aging: Rethinking Retirement and Non-Retirement in a Changing World
by Marjory Zoet Bankson 6 x 9, 160 pp, Quality PB, 978-1-59473-281-2 **$16.99**

Keeping Spiritual Balance as We Grow Older: More than 65 Creative Ways to Use Purpose, Prayer, and the Power of Spirit to Build a Meaningful Retirement
by Molly and Bernie Srode 8 x 8, 224 pp, Quality PB, 978-1-59473-042-9 **$16.99**

Hearing the Call across Traditions: Readings on Faith and Service
Edited by Adam Davis; Foreword by Eboo Patel
6 x 9, 352 pp, Quality PB, 978-1-59473-303-1 **$18.99**; HC, 978-1-59473-264-5 **$29.99**

Honoring Motherhood: Prayers, Ceremonies & Blessings
Edited and with Introductions by Lynn L. Caruso
5 x 7¼, 272 pp, Quality PB, 978-1-58473-384-0 **$9.99**; HC, 978-1-59473-239-3 **$19.99**

The Losses of Our Lives: The Sacred Gifts of Renewal in Everyday Loss
by Dr. Nancy Copeland-Payton 6 x 9, 192 pp, HC, 978-1-59473-271-3 **$19.99**

Renewal in the Wilderness: A Spiritual Guide to Connecting with God in the Natural World *by John Lionberger*
6 x 9, 176 pp, b/w photos, Quality PB, 978-1-59473-219-5 **$16.99**

Soul Fire: Accessing Your Creativity
by Thomas Ryan, CSP 6 x 9, 160 pp, Quality PB, 978-1-59473-243-0 **$16.99**

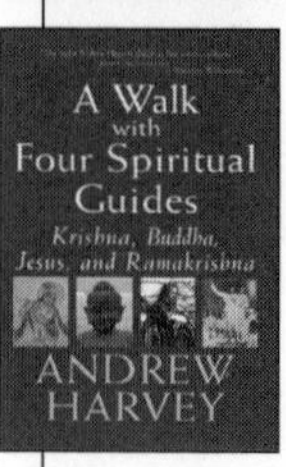

A Spirituality for Brokenness: Discovering Your Deepest Self in Difficult Times
by Terry Taylor 6 x 9, 176 pp, Quality PB, 978-1-59473-229-4 **$16.99**

A Walk with Four Spiritual Guides: Krishna, Buddha, Jesus, and Ramakrishna
by Andrew Harvey 5½ x 8½, 192 pp, b/w photos & illus., Quality PB, 978-1-59473-138-9 **$15.99**

The Workplace and Spirituality: New Perspectives on Research and Practice
Edited by Dr. Joan Marques, Dr. Satinder Dhiman and Dr. Richard King
6 x 9, 256 pp, HC, 978-1-59473-260-7 **$29.99**

Spiritual Practice

Fly-Fishing—The Sacred Art: Casting a Fly as a Spiritual Practice
by Rabbi Eric Eisenkramer and Rev. Michael Attas, MD; Foreword by Chris Wood, CEO, Trout Unlimited; Preface by Lori Simon, executive director, Casting for Recovery
Shares what fly-fishing can teach you about reflection, awe and wonder; the benefits of solitude; the blessing of community and the search for the Divine.
5½ x 8½, 160 pp, Quality PB, 978-1-59473-299-7 **$16.99**

***Lectio Divina*—The Sacred Art:** Transforming Words & Images into Heart-Centered Prayer *by Christine Valters Paintner, PhD*
Expands the practice of sacred reading beyond scriptural texts and makes it accessible in contemporary life. 5½ x 8½, 240 pp, Quality PB, 978-1-59473-300-0 **$16.99**

Writing—The Sacred Art: Beyond the Page to Spiritual Practice
By Rami Shapiro and Aaron Shapiro
Push your writing through the trite and the boring to something fresh, something transformative. Includes over fifty unique, practical exercises.
5½ x 8½, 192 pp, Quality PB, 978-1-59473-372-7 **$16.99**

Dance—The Sacred Art: The Joy of Movement as a Spiritual Practice
by Cynthia Winton-Henry 5½ x 8½, 224 pp, Quality PB, 978-1-59473-268-3 **$16.99**

Everyday Herbs in Spiritual Life: A Guide to Many Practices
by Michael J. Caduto; Foreword by Rosemary Gladstar
7 x 9, 208 pp, 20+ b/w illus., Quality PB, 978-1-59473-174-7 **$16.99**

Giving—The Sacred Art: Creating a Lifestyle of Generosity
by Lauren Tyler Wright 5½ x 8½, 208 pp, Quality PB, 978-1-59473-224-9 **$16.99**

Haiku—The Sacred Art: A Spiritual Practice in Three Lines
by Margaret D. McGee 5½ x 8½, 192 pp, Quality PB, 978-1-59473-269-0 **$16.99**

Hospitality—The Sacred Art: Discovering the Hidden Spiritual Power of Invitation and Welcome *by Rev. Nanette Sawyer; Foreword by Rev. Dirk Ficca*
5½ x 8½, 208 pp, Quality PB, 978-1-59473-228-7 **$16.99**

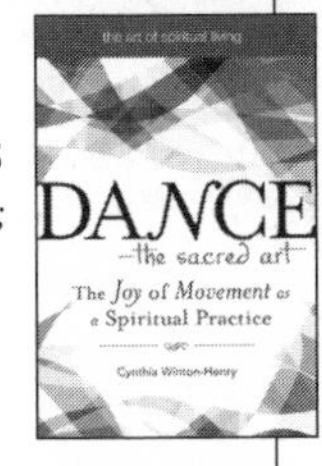

Labyrinths from the Outside In: Walking to Spiritual Insight—A Beginner's Guide
by Donna Schaper and Carole Ann Camp
6 x 9, 208 pp, b/w illus. and photos, Quality PB, 978-1-893361-18-8 **$16.95**

Practicing the Sacred Art of Listening: A Guide to Enrich Your Relationships and Kindle Your Spiritual Life *by Kay Lindahl* 8 x 8, 176 pp, Quality PB, 978-1-893361-85-0 **$16.95**

Recovery—The Sacred Art: The Twelve Steps as Spiritual Practice *by Rami Shapiro; Foreword by Joan Borysenko, PhD* 5½ x 8½, 240 pp, Quality PB, 978-1-59473-259-1 **$16.99**

Running—The Sacred Art: Preparing to Practice *by Dr. Warren A. Kay; Foreword by Kristin Armstrong* 5½ x 8½, 160 pp, Quality PB, 978-1-59473-227-0 **$16.99**

The Sacred Art of Chant: Preparing to Practice
by Ana Hernández 5½ x 8½, 192 pp, Quality PB, 978-1-59473-036-8 **$16.99**

The Sacred Art of Fasting: Preparing to Practice
by Thomas Ryan, CSP 5½ x 8½, 192 pp, Quality PB, 978-1-59473-078-8 **$15.99**

The Sacred Art of Forgiveness: Forgiving Ourselves and Others through God's Grace
by Marcia Ford 8 x 8, 176 pp, Quality PB, 978-1-59473-175-4 **$18.99**

The Sacred Art of Listening: Forty Reflections for Cultivating a Spiritual Practice
by Kay Lindahl; Illus. by Amy Schnapper 8 x 8, 160 pp, b/w illus., Quality PB, 978-1-893361-44-7 **$16.99**

The Sacred Art of Lovingkindness: Preparing to Practice
by Rabbi Rami Shapiro; Foreword by Marcia Ford 5½ x 8½, 176 pp, Quality PB, 978-1-59473-151-8 **$16.99**

Sacred Attention: A Spiritual Practice for Finding God in the Moment
by Margaret D. McGee 6 x 9, 144 pp, Quality PB, 978-1-59473-291-1 **$16.99**

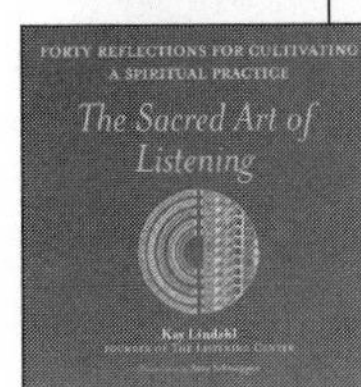

Soul Fire: Accessing Your Creativity
by Thomas Ryan, CSP 6 x 9, 160 pp, Quality PB, 978-1-59473-243-0 **$16.99**

Spiritual Adventures in the Snow: Skiing & Snowboarding as Renewal for Your Soul
by Dr. Marcia McFee and Rev. Karen Foster; Foreword by Paul Arthur
5½ x 8½, 208 pp, Quality PB, 978-1-59473-270-6 **$16.99**

Thanking & Blessing—The Sacred Art: Spiritual Vitality through Gratefulness
by Jay Marshall, PhD; Foreword by Philip Gulley 5½ x 8½, 176 pp, Quality PB, 978-1-59473-231-7 **$16.99**

About SKYLIGHT PATHS Publishing

SkyLight Paths Publishing is creating a place where people of different spiritual traditions come together for challenge and inspiration, a place where we can help each other understand the mystery that lies at the heart of our existence.

Through spirituality, our religious beliefs are increasingly becoming a part of our lives—rather than *apart* from our lives. While many of us may be more interested than ever in spiritual growth, we may be less firmly planted in traditional religion. Yet, we do want to deepen our relationship to the sacred, to learn from our own as well as from other faith traditions, and to practice in new ways.

SkyLight Paths sees both believers and seekers as a community that increasingly transcends traditional boundaries of religion and denomination—people wanting to learn from each other, *walking together, finding the way.*

For your information and convenience, at the back of this book we have provided a list of other SkyLight Paths books you might find interesting and useful. They cover the following subjects:

Buddhism / Zen
Catholicism
Children's Books
Christianity
Comparative Religion
Current Events
Earth-Based Spirituality
Enneagram
Global Spiritual Perspectives
Gnosticism
Hinduism / Vedanta
Inspiration
Islam / Sufism
Judaism
Kabbalah
Meditation
Midrash Fiction
Monasticism
Mysticism
Poetry
Prayer
Religious Etiquette
Retirement
Spiritual Biography
Spiritual Direction
Spirituality
Women's Interest
Worship

Or phone, fax, mail or e-mail to: SKYLIGHT PATHS Publishing
Sunset Farm Offices, Route 4 • P.O. Box 237 • Woodstock, Vermont 05091
Tel: (802) 457-4000 • Fax: (802) 457-4004 • www.skylightpaths.com
Credit card orders: (800) 962-4544 (8:30AM–5:30PM EST Monday–Friday)